# WHEN
# SOMEONE YOU
# LOVE IS ANGRY

# WHEN SOMEONE YOU LOVE IS ANGRY

A 7-Step Program for Dealing

with Toxic Anger and Taking Back

Control of Your Life

W. DOYLE GENTRY, Ph.D.

BERKLEY BOOKS, NEW YORK

**THE BERKLEY PUBLISHING GROUP**
**Published by the Penguin Group**
**Penguin Group (USA) Inc.**
**375 Hudson Street, New York, New York 10014, USA**
Penguin Group (Canada), 10 Alcorn Avenue, Toronto, Ontario M4V 3B2, Canada
(a division of Pearson Penguin Canada Inc.)
Penguin Books Ltd., 80 Strand, London WC2R 0RL, England
Penguin Group Ireland, 25 St. Stephen's Green, Dublin 2, Ireland
(a division of Penguin Books, Ltd.)
Penguin Group (Australia), 250 Camberwell Road, Camberwell, Victoria 3124,
Australia (a division of Pearson Australia Group Pty. Ltd.)
Penguin Books India Pvt. Ltd., 11 Community Centre, Panchsheel Park,
New Delhi—110 017, India
Penguin Group (NZ), Cnr. Airborne and Rosedale Roads, Albany, Auckland 1310,
New Zealand
(a division of Pearson New Zealand Ltd.)
Penguin Books (South Africa) (Pty.) Ltd., 24 Sturdee Avenue, Rosebank,
Johannesburg 2196, South Africa

Penguin Books Ltd., Registered Offices: 80 Strand, London WC2R 0RL, England

This book is an original publication of The Berkley Publishing Group.

PRINTING HISTORY
Berkley trade paperback edition / September 2004

Library of Congress Cataloging-in-Publication Data

Gentry, W. Doyle (William Doyle), 1943–
When someone you love is angry / W. Doyle Gentry.
p. cm.
Includes bibliographical references.
ISBN 0-425-19811-1
1. Anger. I. Title.

RC569.5.A53G46 2004
152.4'7—dc22                    2004050504

PRINTED IN THE UNITED STATES OF AMERICA

10  9  8  7  6  5  4  3  2  1

# ACKNOWLEDGMENTS

Writing a book is a solitary endeavor, but one that cannot be accomplished without help. As such, I need to thank a number of people. First, I am indebted to Denise Silvestro, my editor at Penguin, for taking on this project and for her "critical eye" in the revision stage. She was a true collaborator and she shares the credit for whatever measure of success this book achieves. Second, I appreciate the hard work of my agent, Denise Marcil, and her able associate, Maura Kye, who guided me through every step of the publication process in a rather seamless fashion. I trust this will be the beginning of a long and fruitful partnership. I am grateful to my loving family—Catherine, Rebecca, and Christopher—for their unconditional love and support, as always, in this and all other facets of my long career. Without them, everything lacks meaning and possibility. Finally, and most of all, I express my heartfelt thanks to the men and women, whose names and identifying characteristics have been altered to protect their privacy, who have eagerly shared their personal stories of having endured "loving but angry" relationships, even when the retelling of such stories proved upsetting. I was personally moved by each and every one of them in ways I never anticipated. Thank you all.

To my mother,

*Mary B. Gentry,*

who taught me a lot about

anger and love

*"How much more grievous are the consequences of anger*
*than the causes of it."*
*Marcus Aurelius*

# CONTENTS

# PREFACE

The main focus of this book is anger, not love. I consider the issue of love here only because experiencing anger within the context of a loving relationship represents a truly special circumstance—especially for the person on the receiving end of all that anger.

Like anger, and all other emotions for that matter, love is illogical. It is true that we humans literally "fall in love," without rhyme or reason, just as we suddenly and inextricably find ourselves in a state of anger. The origins of love and anger are at the same time unconscious and complex, and it is only in retrospect that we seek to impose logic and rationality on such feelings. Robert Redford's character, Tom Booker, in the movie *The Horse Whisperer* expresses the fallacy of trying to make sense out of love when he explains his feelings for his ex-wife by saying, "I didn't love her because it was right. I just loved her."

As we shall see in this book, anger in loving relationships constitutes a special circumstance by virtue of the fact that the love we feel for that other person—boyfriend, brother, parent, child, spouse—can block any chance of escape we have from their abusive anger. It is different from non-loving relationships—co-workers, neighbors, strangers—in which one can simply distance oneself from the other person's ill temper, if need be, by terminating the relationship altogether. But how does a mother distance herself from her raging eight-year-old son? How easy is it for a woman to leave a man she has loved for over twenty years even though he abuses her emotionally day after day? How does one deal with abusive anger in an elderly parent, a sibling, or the first "real love" of your life? These are but some of the tough questions we will address in this book.

Love is, by definition, an attractive emotion. Love pulls us toward other human beings—physically, emotionally, and spiritually—just as surely as gravity keeps us anchored to this earth. Love bonds us and makes us the social animals that we are. Anger, on the other hand, is a repulsive emotion. Anger pushes us away from those we love. Because of its power to alienate others, anger becomes an antisocial emotion. Love strives for intimacy; anger, for separation. Those of us who are involved in what I refer to throughout this book as "loving but angry" (LBA) relationships know all too well the inherent conflict and emotional paralysis imposed on us by this type of push-pull relationship and the unfortunate, unhealthy consequences that ensue.

Contrary to what most of us may believe, it *is* possible to love an angry person. For many years, as a mental health professional, I thought this was wrong. It was inconceivable to me, for example, that a battered woman could continue to love an angry, abusive boyfriend or husband. For that matter, I had never understood why my mother continued to love my father after being subjected to years of violent anger, long after their divorce and his subsequent death. I had been trained to think that it was a woman's fear, her dependent (or codependent) nature, her lack of self-esteem, or her abiding sense of learned helplessness that caused her to return willingly and repeatedly to an abusive relationship, not love. Who in their right mind, I asked myself, could possibly love anyone who had hurt them beyond words or who, worse yet, might someday kill them? There had to be some explanation, something lacking in these women that rendered them victims of domestic violence. I now concede that such "old school" thinking was naive and misguided—and it most assuredly did not help those poor women. My advice to terminate these relationships was, I now understand, just as illogical to these women as their seemingly self-destructive behavior was to me. What held these women to these abusive relationships was love and some of the misguided, mythical beliefs that we explore later in the book, beliefs like, "if an angry person loves me enough, he/she will change."

While my years of counseling clients of all types who are suffering from "angry but loving" relationships have educated me about the illogical, albeit powerful nature of human love, I still do not believe love by itself provides an adequate rationale (excuse) for tolerating abusive anger. To tolerate harmful, abusive anger in any relationship, even a loving one, is, in a word, to be a victim. And my whole purpose of writing *When Someone You Love Is Angry* is to teach you how not to be victimized when you find yourself stuck in an LBA relationship.

So, what should you do? How can you recover from the damage

you have already suffered from your loved one's anger or, better yet, how can you set your life on a healthier course in the future? As this book will suggest, there are no simple answers to such questions; nevertheless, it is possible to achieve that end.

There is actually very little advice out there for people who are on the receiving end of another person's "toxic" anger. Almost without exception, the advice that is available is specifically directed at the angry person rather than at his/her victims; it tends to focus on persons other than loved ones; or it is limited to readers who have been physically battered at the hands of a loved one, primarily a spouse. Unfortunately, the latter only accounts for about 10 percent of cases in which someone suffers because of another person's anger.

Traditionally, the consensus has been that victims of abusive anger have but four options: (1) wait, pray, and hope that the angry partner will change; (2) take it upon yourself to change the angry partner; (3) terminate the relationship with your angry partner as quickly and safely as you can; and, (4) seek professional help as a last resort. In my more than three decades of working with abuse victims, I have concluded that most, by far, choose option (1)—the "wait, pray, and hope" approach—and that, by doing so, they invite further harm to themselves. Edith, a pleasant fifty-one-year-old retired schoolteacher, found this out the hard way. She married when she was only nineteen years old, and on her wedding night she found out just what kind of man her husband really was—after he got drunk, flew into a rage, and sexually assaulted, and then beat her. When she went to her family shortly thereafter and told them about her husband's daily fits of anger, they were unsympathetic, saying only "You made your bed, now lie in it!" And so she did for eighteen long, painful years, waiting and hoping, until, at age thirty-seven, she finally left him for the safety of a solitary lifestyle with no thought of ever remarrying. To this day, a decade and a half later, Edith continues to be haunted by recurrent, vivid dreams of horrific violence—being beaten by a baseball bat, scalded, cussed at, and demeaned in full view of her children—all at the hands of a very angry man with whom she just happened to fall in love. Edith had not chosen to marry an angry man; on the contrary, her husband had successfully managed to hide that part of his true self until after they were married. But marry an angry man she did, and she spent eighteen years of her life hoping he would change.

Option (2)—trying to "fix" the angry loved one—is also a popular choice among victims of abusive anger. Unfortunately, for a number of reasons which I will spell out in this book, this rarely, if ever, resolves the problem. Angry people stay angry unless they decide to change, and regrettably, few do.

Option (3) asks, Why not end an LBA relationship as quickly as you can? Lots of reasons, actually. To begin with, you love that other person, and because of that you are stuck. Secondly, one cannot simply choose to walk away from all types of LBA relationships; think of parents of angry children or adult children of elderly, angry parents for whom they are responsible. Where one could conceivably terminate a relationship with an angry loved one, other factors come into play. Some, like Edith, stay because they are encouraged to do so by the very people they go to for help. Others are reluctant to admit they made a mistake in their choice of partners. Still others are ashamed to acknowledge that they have been victims of physical and emotional abuse. Many are afraid—with good reason—that their angry partner will become even more rageful and hurt them even more if they try to leave. Some are eternal optimists, firmly convinced that they have the ultimate power to transform their loved one's temperament. And some are simply too loyal for their own good. Whatever the reason, they remain in harm's way.

Fewer yet exercise option (4)—seeking professional help—at least not in time to prevent extensive damage. Unfortunately, we still live in a culture in which counseling carries a certain stigma— a service provided only to the weak among us, the inadequate, and those lacking in heart. To make matters worse, we also find ourselves in an era of so-called "managed care" (which translates to "managed costs"), which has rather successfully limited access of even insured persons to mental health care. Ironically, most of the clients whom I have treated for abusive anger, in fact, come to me initially complaining of other problems. Two of the stories I will offer in subsequent chapters, for example, tell of middle-aged men who came for counseling because they were depressed, only to find that the source of their mood disorder had to do with a chronically abusive father and a rageful, vengeful wife.

*When Someone You Love Is Angry* offers readers a viable fifth alternative, one that goes beyond passively "waiting and praying" but stops short of seeking professional help. Rather, it offers a unique seven-step program of self-help strategies which, when followed as directed, have proven to be universally effective in reducing the toxicity of LBA relationships. Its success lies in the fact that the approach is based on sound scientific principles of human behavior as well as "true life" testimonials from people just like yourself, who once found themselves victimized by a loved one's malevolent anger, but who have since managed to navigate their way to a safer, healthier existence.

Any effort to change your behavior, whether you're dealing with acoholism, cigarette smoking, obesity, or compulsive gambling, requires an adequate support system or else you will at best enjoy only short-lived success and will ultimately be doomed to failure. So readers must first identify an ally or support team in their effort to recover from the damage inflicted by the LBA relationship. Readers must next explore the labyrinth of common mental traps that have kept them from taking proactive steps to resolve the opposing emotions of love and anger that together define LBA relationships. I call this "getting your mind right." Third, it is imperative that limits be set on your loved one's toxic anger both as a measure of damage control and as a means of corrective feedback for the angry partner. Next, participants in the LBA relationship must come to realize that relationship anger—whether with a spouse, child, parent, sibling, or friend—is, by definition, a two-way street. Readers will learn how not to unwittingly facilitate the harmful emotional behavior (rage) which will ultimately be directed squarely at them. Similarly, readers must learn not to "answer anger with anger," perhaps the most difficult lesson of all. For, to do so only escalates the cycle of interpersonal anger. Sixth, readers must develop and implement a program of stress-inoculation training to mitigate the situation-specific stresses that accompany relationship anger. And, lastly, readers who ultimately find it necessary to terminate an LBA relationship (when all else fails) will find it easier to make a clean and orderly break with loved ones if they have made a concerted, good faith effort to salvage the LBA relationship by executing the preceding six steps. They will then not spend the remainder of their lives plagued by self-doubts (and recrimination) about, "What if I had just . . . ?"

It's now time to get to work. Good luck!

CHAPTER ONE

# YOUR LOVE, THEIR ANGER

Over the past thirty years, I have listened to the personal stories of literally thousands of people who, like an estimated twenty million other Americans, suffer from "toxic" anger—anger that is experienced far too often, is far too intense, and lasts far too long. I have also listened to the stories of their victims, most of whom were, in fact, loved ones. And this is what I have learned:

One of the chief emotional consequences of toxic anger is a profound feeling of sadness for the angry person as well as for those on the receiving end of this burdensome emotion. This sadness results not only for what was, or is (abuse, alienation), but more importantly for what otherwise might have been—the loss of harmony and a feeling of connectedness with those closest to us. In that sense, toxic anger acts like a thief, robbing us of the intimacy we long to share with others. Toxic anger, especially if it is experienced early in life, during the formative years, usually leaves lifelong emotional scars. Toxic anger has the power to transform and pervert personality in all those who experience it personally or as one of its victims. Toxic anger is contagious—that is, the early victims of toxic anger often become perpetrators of rage later on. And toxic anger can be lethal.

———

Jerry is forty-three years old, married, a police officer, and father of two teenage daughters. He lives in the same town as his parents, whom he visits frequently, but he hasn't had contact with his only brother, Sam, for the past seven years. This estrangement from a close family member whom he continues to love, but will not reach out to, is a source of profound sadness for him. You can hear it in his voice when he talks about their years together growing up.

"Sam will never know how much I admired and respected him when we were young. He was good looking, popular with all the kids, strong, and athletic. Who wouldn't want to be *his* little brother? He was my hero."

But, unfortunately, Sam had a dark side—a tendency toward sudden, explosive anger. "He had no tolerance, no patience, for his dislikes. Everything had to be his way. You couldn't disagree with him or discuss anything. He'd rant and rave for hours," Jerry noted, recalling that his brother's rage often escalated to a point of physical violence. He poignantly recounts one morning at breakfast, when the two were still in high school, having to "pull a knife on Sam" just to keep from getting hurt. "His eyes would get real beady, and then you had better look out! Oh, he'd always say he was sorry afterward, but the damage was already done."

This pattern of love and anger between the brothers continued from the time they were six or eight years old until they last saw each other sometime in their thirties. "Sam's temper got worse with each passing year," Jerry explained, "so our relationship never grew. He was always the angry older brother and I was the scared little brother, and I'm sure that's how it would be if we saw each other again today."

"How did your brother's rage affect you?" I asked.

"It made me, at a very early age, skeptical of people, more suspicious than normal, less open, less accepting of others than I'd like to be. It's made me work hard to keep my family circle really small."

As is often the case, it also helped Jerry become a very angry man in his own right. His wife is quick to point out, "You can't talk to him; he gets mad when you don't see things his way—just like his brother—and he closes the door on any further discussion." The only difference between the two is that Sam expressed his rage outwardly through screaming and violence, whereas Jerry retreats inwardly into angry silence, where he can remain for days, shutting himself off from everyone around him.

This combination of cynicism and suppressed anger, which originates from his early LBA relationship, was, in fact, a major contributing factor to Jerry's sudden heart attack six months earlier, which almost cost him his life. "We don't have any heart disease in our family and I don't smoke, so everyone, including me, was left wondering where this came from." Numerous studies have shown rather convincingly that toxic anger, whether suppressed or expressed, is linked to a greater risk for coronary heart disease and subsequent heart attacks and that this additional risk is independent of other well-known factors such as cigarette smoking, obesity, sedentary lifestyle, and high blood pressure.[1]

Jerry's conflict over how he feels about his brother continues despite their years of separation. He mostly avoids the issue by not thinking or talking about Sam. But when asked, he is clearly angry over the fact that "anger stole my big brother from me!" Ironically, it is the love he still feels for Sam that causes him to keep his distance. "I don't want to risk the five or six good memories I have of him." If he saw his brother again and Sam was his old angry self, Jerry adds, "I would lose even those and then I'd feel like I never had a brother at all." And, that's a risk he is not about to take.

———————

Toxic anger in children and adolescents makes effective parenting virtually impossible. Parents of overly angry children feel compelled to defend their young no matter how badly they behave—because they love them. The range of emotions that ensue from LBA parent-child relationships is endless.

Toxic anger is on the rise among today's youth, and parents who come from an earlier generation with different "rules of engagement" are at a loss as to how to cope with such behavior. Our own survey findings of regional schools suggest that nearly half (47 percent) of middle-school children openly admit to excessive anger, and almost one in five (18 percent) report experiencing rage on a daily basis. Toxic anger can defeat even parents with the best, and most loving, of intentions. Sometimes, the best way to help a child who suffers from toxic anger is to quit trying to help them. And there should be no "special rules" for dealing with anger in those closest to us.

————

When Sherri, the mother of a sixteen-year-old adolescent boy I had been seeing for anger management for the past year, says, "It hasn't been easy raising him," she grossly underestimates the psychological impact her son's temper has had on her. This muted response, in part, reflects her continued reluctance—even though she admits she feels abused—to say anything too negative about this young man whom she dearly loves.

The truth of the matter is, however, that her son's frequent "anger fits"—yelling, cursing, ripping the phone out of the wall, knocking holes in doors when he doesn't get his way—have taken their emotional toll. "You have the whole spectrum of emotions. You become very angry; you get hysterical; you feel absolutely devastated at times; and, you have enormous feelings of guilt. I found myself asking over and over, 'What have I done to create this?'"

Sherri, like most parents of angry children, was completely unprepared to cope with a child who showed signs of outrageous behavior from as early as age three. "I came from a generation where children were seen and not heard. I had never witnessed anyone— not my brothers, not my sisters, and certainly not me—who would say or do the angry things my son does right to my face."

Sherri and her husband did the best they could for their son. "We made a lot of mistakes, I'm sure, but lately I think we've finally begun to do a few things right." The biggest change, and one that came only after a decade of failed attempts to correct her son's behavior, is that Sherri has learned to emotionally detach from her son's anger as a self-protective maneuver. "I've told my son that life is full of choices and along with those choices go consequences. Rage, as I now see it, is a choice. If that's how he wants to live his life, okay, then live it that way." This new way of thinking about their son's toxic anger runs counter to the normal parental instinct to both protect and "fix" a child's aberrant behavior, which is why it takes so long to develop. It seems that one must first exhaust that instinct before one can consider alternative ways of dealing with the problem.

Sherri is no longer trying to "fix" her son's emotional life. As with alcoholism, she now understands that much of what she did, albeit with the best of intentions, to curb her son's anger was actually enabling him to perpetuate the problem. She has also learned that one can be a good parent, and a loving parent, without being a victim of emotional abuse. "I'm not giving up on my son, but I am relinquishing control of his emotional life to him—where it rightfully belongs." For example, in the past, Sherri would drop whatever she was doing during the day, even at her job, to come home and rescue her son from one of his tantrums. She no longer does that, leaving him instead the job of calming himself down and/or paying the consequences for any destruction that results from his momentary rage.

Sherri has learned to apply the same set of standards for acceptable conduct to her son that she would use with people with whom she does not have a loving relationship. "There's no one else on this earth that I would stay around for more than two minutes if they treated me the way he does. So, now, when he acts that way, I just turn and walk away. I won't tolerate it!" Having a single set of standards for how to deal with other people's anger, while awkward at first, became second nature to Sherri and her husband much more quickly than one might imagine.

When asked if this "about-face" on her part affected her son's outrageous behavior, she is quick to note, "Well, he's not perfect. But we haven't had any real violent episodes for over a year now. Things are better."

———

Toxic anger is often an intergenerational problem in families. One reason is that parents and children often share the same temperament; also children learn to handle their emotions the way their parents do. When I first began to work with angry adolescents, a colleague of mine who is a child psychologist suggested that I always ask the angry youngster, "Who else in the family has a bad temper?" Invariably, the child can identify at least one parent who shares this problem, most often the father. Angry fathers tend to produce, in effect, angry sons. One estimate is that anywhere from one-fourth to one-third of families witness episodes of violent anger on a regular basis.[2] And, as the example below illustrates, the effects of such exposure can be devastating to all concerned.

———

Donald came to see me several years ago for treatment of a midlife depression after being fired from a job he both loved and was good at for well over a decade. While trying to help him work through that problem, I quickly realized that he also suffered from a case of long-standing, serious parental anger.

"Most people like my father, actually think of him as a sweet man, but they don't see his underlying anger like I do. He's not one to get upset, comment on it, and then move on. He lets things build up, keeps it all inside, and then the lid blows off and he explodes." Since his mother passed away five years ago and his sister moved to another city, Donald is on the receiving end of most of his father's rage.

"Every time we get into one of those conversations and he ends up blowing up, I ask myself, 'What did I do?' All I'm trying to do is help him calm down, see things more rationally, and this is the thanks I get!"

How has this pattern of repeated anger affected Donald? It has left him with an abiding anger at his father: "I feel like 'to hell with him.' I don't want to have anything to do with him. I want him to go on home, to leave me alone. To leave my wife alone. To leave my kids alone. The last blow-up we had was months ago and, yes, I'm still angry at him."

This mutual anger also leaves Donald feeling alienated from the only parent he has left. "My father's anger has so consumed him that the person he was is now lost somewhere in there. I feel orphaned, because he's not there for me anymore."

Perhaps most important, it has left Donald struggling to hang on to a love he felt for his father because of all the support and encouragement he provided in his early years growing up. "He and my mother were always there for us, praising us when we did well in school, helping us with scouts and sports, making sure our self-esteem was bolstered. But these last twenty years, quite honestly, it's been tough trying to keep loving him. I'd be lying if I didn't admit that his anger has tainted our relationship."

Interestingly, having said all this, if you ask Donald if his father was ever abusive, he would without hesitation answer, "No."

———

Women remain the more likely victims of toxic anger. Women between ages fifteen and forty-four are more likely, in fact, to experience abusive anger in a domestic relationship than they are to be mugged by a stranger, be involved in an automobile accident, or die of cancer.[3] Unfortunately, millions have their first encounter with abusive anger during their adolescent and early adult years within the context of "first love" relationships. The problem is, in fact, so pervasive that social scientists have recently coined a term for the phenomenon—*intimate partner violence* (IPV).[4] Young women are particularly vulnerable to rageful behavior at this early point in their lives for a number of reasons. Many come from happy, anger-free homes and thus they are unprepared to deal effectively with such behavior. Also, since their identities are not fully developed, they tend to accept blame for the anger being expressed by their loved one. One sign, in fact, that a young woman may be experiencing IPV is if she spends an inordinate amount of time trying to "fix" (or change) herself in an effort to improve the relationship. And, lastly, many are more afraid of abandonment in this first significant outside-the-family emotional relationship than they are for their own personal safety. As I will discuss later on, the damage from these early LBA relationships can be serious, even life threatening.

———

Even though it has now been a year since Sarah, an attractive twenty-year-old college student, ended her relationship with her boyfriend, Todd, she continues to experience the aftershock of this turbulent "first love" relationship.

"Tell me about the relationship," I asked.

"We were together fifteen months, and things were good at first. He started out being a nice guy. But, then—after about six months—we got into this pattern where we couldn't be in the same room together for more than five minutes without him getting angry at something I was doing and then we'd start fighting."

"Did he ever get to the point of physical violence?"

"No, I wouldn't say that he had that toxic anger you talk about. But he would yell and belittle me—you know, like I was the bad part of the relationship, that it was my fault he was always so angry."

"He was like that every day, every time you got together, and you didn't think his anger was toxic?"

"Right. He wasn't violent; he just yelled at me, would continue to yell, and then walk out."

"Had you ever been exposed to this kind of everyday anger before?"

"Absolutely not," she said "My parents had a strong relationship, and I only remember my father getting angry with my mother once all the time I was growing up."

"How did you feel when that happened?"

"I was scared that he wouldn't come back, that our relationship was over. But he did come back."

"And, did you feel that same way—frightened—when Todd got real angry and walked out on you all those times?"

"Now that you mention it, I suppose I did. I would immediately think, 'Oh my God, it's over!' and I would try to 'fix' the situation—by fixing me. You know, I was beginning to believe what he was saying, that I was the reason he was always losing his temper."

The emotional trauma of having loved someone who was always angry left Sarah, a year later, afraid of entering into another serious relationship and highly sensitive about being in the company of anyone who shows even the slightest hint of being irritated. "Todd would always get quiet just before he got angry and started in on me. So, now, when I'm out with someone and he gets quiet or seems not to like something I've said or done, I leave and don't look back. He won't hear from me again!"

---

Toxic anger, within the context of LBA relationships, is not synonymous with physical violence. More often than not, it expresses itself through emotional violence—verbal outbursts, insults, threats—all attempts to demean and intimidate the object of one's anger. The damage that results from such emotional "battering" is, however, no less hurtful and lasting. At sixty years of age, I can still remember that day when I was eight years old and my mother, who could be a very loving person, said to me in a state of rage, "I hate you. I wish you had never been born!" I wish she had just hit me— it would have hurt a lot less.

———————

Marilyn is not your typical battered wife. She has no bruises or broken bones to show for her many years of marriage to a man "who was angry all the time about almost everything." But her life and health has been greatly affected nevertheless.

Marilyn is recently divorced at age forty-four. Surprisingly, she still loves her husband; she just doesn't like him anymore. "His anger didn't make me quit loving him. If it had, it would have been much easier to leave."

Her husband, Donnie, was constantly irritable and prone to frequent episodes of explosive verbal rage. His outbursts could come at any moment, and Marilyn was ever alert to the possibility of an impending tantrum. In fact, when asked what had changed since her divorce, she quickly replied, "I feel absolutely relieved every time I walk through the front door of my apartment and don't have to worry about seeing that angry face staring back at me."

Another positive change is that Marilyn is no longer an angry person herself. "I never wanted anger to be part of my life," she said, "but that was part of him." She had been raised by an angry, alcoholic father—who she also loved very much—and the last thing she needed was a relationship with yet another angry man. "But when Donnie would lash out at me, I could never let it be. Getting angry back at him was my way of making a statement: You're not going to get away with this!"

The fact that her husband's rage did not last long was hardly a consolation. "He was fine after he blew up, but I wasn't." Most often, after one of her own tantrums, Marilyn was left with feelings of shame and self-recrimination, which lasted for days and invariably led to a migraine headache, an affliction she suffered throughout their marriage.

Why did Marilyn stay in this loving but angry relationship so long? Two reasons: "At first, I kept telling myself it would get better, but it didn't. Then, as time went on, I wanted to leave but I had nowhere to go. I couldn't take care of myself and those three children."

Her overview of the life she shared with her ex-husband: "Looking back, his anger put me in a bad place. All the time we were married, I felt like I was a caretaker for an angry, adult child."

For Marilyn, "life is simplified now." She is free to live without feeling the weight of the world on her shoulders.

———

Women are not the only victims of toxic anger. A recent report indicates that an estimated 800,000 men are subjected to spousal abuse annually.[5] This number most likely grossly underestimates what may well be a growing "silent minority" of males struggling in relationships with very angry girlfriends, sisters, wives, and mothers. I recall some years ago attending a men's workshop hosted by the poet and writer Robert Bly and being impressed by the cathartic public testimony of one man after another as to the emotional, physical, and even sexual abuse they had suffered at the hands of their angry, controlling, albeit loving mothers. The suppressed rage that was apparent in these men was alarming, to say the least. In our macho society, who would have imagined that men could be so hurt by women they love?

———————

Victor, a middle-aged executive, sat in my office in tears, distraught, and said simply, "I'm at the end of my endurance with my wife's anger." He has tried, unsuccessfully, for ten years to deal with her incessant angry accusations, both in public and private, and her loud, intimidating behavior. What makes his story even more compelling is the fact that Victor is a "man's man," someone who throughout his life has embraced all sorts of physical challenges—mountain climbing, sailing, motorcycling. And yet, here he sat in obvious emotional pain, feeling totally hopeless, and fearful of what might happen if he and his wife have one more angry encounter.

Like most men who suffer abuse from women, Victor waited too long before seeking help. He was concerned that others might see him as "weak" and, again like most men, he firmly believed that he somehow should be able to fix his wife's rage in much the same way he would repair a leaky faucet or a broken railing on his deck.

Over the years, Victor had tried everything he could think of to assuage his wife's recurring anger. He tried "not saying anything when she lit in on me." He tried avoiding her by working long hours to minimize their time together. He tried being logical, calmly defending himself against each one of her unfounded accusations. He had gotten angry with her. He had even tried "barricading myself in the bedroom." But, her angry monologues about his alleged infidelity, dishonesty, and general ineptitude continued unabated.

And what about the love he felt for his wife during the early years of their marriage? "I know I should love her," he says rather sadly, "but there's nothing there anymore. As far as I'm concerned, she's dead."

That's what I meant when I said Victor had waited too long.

————

Finally, as the last story illustrates, toxic anger is also evident within same-sex partnerships. No matter how one judges the morality of such intimate relationships, love is still love and anger is still anger. And when these two powerful emotions come into conflict, the damage that results is the same.

————

Tony came from a faraway state to spend a day consulting with me about anger—not his, but rather that of his male partner and lover of the past seven years. "Living with my friend, Alan, is like living on top of a volcano. I never know when he is going to erupt next, so I live always with one eye in the back of my head. Even when we have good times together, it's hard to trust that they will last."

Tony is not only an emotionally battered man, he has experienced repeated physical abuse as well. "I've wound up in the emergency room more than once."

Tony is mystified by his partner's emotional outbursts: "There's no logic to it. He can become violent over something as simple as putting the mail in the wrong place." This is, in fact, why Tony made the long trip to visit with me. Like many victims of LBA relationships, he mistakenly believes that if he can just understand why Alan becomes so angry, he can prevent it by knowing what *not* to do. He is looking for a way to be more responsible for his partner's rage.

There is less violence in their relationship these days, but only because Tony took a job in another part of the country and they see each other less. Ironically, it has been during this time of separation that Tony has begun to notice, and accept, just how much rage his friend "carries around inside him—not just about me, about everything."

Tony's current dilemma is whether to reunite with Alan. Part of him wants to stay away, but an equally strong part says, "But I love him and, of course, I keep hoping *next* time we will sort things out, *next* time it will be different."

Tony is also beginning to question his partner's ability to love him in return. "Just because someone becomes angry with you, it doesn't mean they don't love you. But if someone is continuously angry and disruptive in the relationship, then they obviously lack respect for you and mutual respect, for me at least, is a key component to love."

———

The issues raised in these heart-wrenching stories are the subject matter of *When Someone You Love Is Angry*. It is sensitive to the daunting task we face each and every day in trying to juxtapose the two strongest human emotions—love and anger—within a single relationship, while simultaneously trying to minimize the destructive effects such relationships have on feelings of personal safety, levels of emotional intimacy, and your bio-psycho-social health. Reading this book will answer once and for all important questions such as:

- Can toxic anger stunt the growth of an otherwise loving relationship?

- Doesn't just saying you're sorry take away the hurt caused by anger?

- Can I ever hope to have a normal emotional life if I find myself in an LBA relationship?

- Am I becoming an angry person myself as a result of being in an LBA relationship?

- Anger is only toxic when it leads to actual physical violence, right?

- Is it possible to still love someone but not live with them or relate to them on a regular basis because of their anger?

- If I try hard enough, I should be able to fix an LBA relationship, right?

- Can early LBA relationships affect decisions I make throughout the rest of my life?

- Do I really want to spend my whole life being a caretaker for an overly angry person just because I love them?

- Can a loved one's anger make me physically ill?

- How much simpler is life without LBA relationships?

- Must I be a victim of an LBA relationship?

- If I detach from an LBA relationship, does that mean I don't love that person anymore?

- Isn't it true that only women have to worry about being on the receiving end of LBA relationships?

- What must I do to recover emotionally after terminating an LBA relationship?

And, there's more.

## SHOULD I READ THIS BOOK?

If you are still not sure whether you are presently engaged in an LBA relationship, take a minute and answer the questions below as accurately and truthfully as you can.

1. Does your loved one get irritable or angry at least once a day?          YES   NO

2. Would you rate your loved one's anger a 7 or higher on a 10-point scale, ranging from 1 (very mild) to 10 (very intense)?          YES   NO

3. Once mad, does your loved one's anger last for more than half an hour before it subsides?          YES   NO

4. Has your loved one ever pushed, shoved, or hit you in anger?          YES   NO

5. Has your loved one's anger ever left you feeling   YES   NO
   anxious or depressed?

6. Would you say you have become a much angrier   YES   NO
   person since being in this relationship?

7. Has your loved one's anger ever resulted in your   YES   NO
   being sexually abused?

8. Do you find yourself worrying about your loved one's   YES   NO
   temper?

9. Are you beginning to question your love for this   YES   NO
   angry person?

10. Have you sought counseling for problems arising   YES   NO
    out of this relationship?

If you answered YES to even one of these questions, you definitely need to read this book. It is my hope that the chapters that follow will help you identify toxic anger in your loved ones, learn to appreciate why these people are so angry to begin with, understand why you cannot change them, try as you may, and, most importantly, what you can do to steer yourself clear of "harm's way." This book takes you on a journey of personal insight and self-care. In the end, it is really about *your* story, *your* struggle, and what I hope will be *your* success.

# CHAPTER TWO

# HOW ANGRY IS *TOO* ANGRY?

Each time I meet someone who is involved in an LBA relationship, I find myself confronted with four crucial questions that must be answered before you can even begin to deal effectively with a loved one's anger. The first question is: *How angry is too angry?*

Anger is a universal emotion, experienced in some way, shape, or form by all persons living on this earth. There is, in fact, no culture worldwide—ranging from civilized Western societies to primitive, preliterate tribes in Borneo and New Guinea—whose members do not recognize anger as one of a handful of "basic" emotions along with feelings of joy, sadness, and fear.[1]

Anger, on the other hand, is not universal if by that we mean that all human beings experience this unpleasant, at times disruptive, emotion in the same exact way. Of course we don't. To the contrary, some of us experience angry feelings much more often than others and some far more intensely than others. It is these individual differences in the *frequency* and *strength* of our emotional response that determines whether anger is reasonable or "toxic." People also differ in terms of how long *(duration)* they stay mad once they are provoked, but I now believe this dimension of anger is only important in regards to how one expresses the emotion—for example, holding it in by pouting versus letting it out quickly by screaming at someone.

When I ask people to evaluate anger—their own and that of their loved ones—based on their own notions of what is reasonable, they are more likely to underestimate the severity of the problem and they tend to focus on only one dimension of the problem. For example, those who are prone to intense fits of anger are often quick to argue that, "It's not like I lose my temper all the time [frequency]. So, what's the big deal?" Similarly, others who react angrily many times each day will attempt to rationalize their outrageous behavior by virtue of the fact that, "It's not like I fly into a rage [intensity] and lose control, like some people!" To satisfactorily answer the question, "How angry is *too* angry?" I believe it is imperative that you first consider both dimensions of anger simultaneously, and, second, that you have a method of comparing these assessments against some standard of what is normal.

To determine if the person with whom you have a relationship suffers from what I like to call the Toxic Anger Syndrome, all you need to do is answer the following two questions as honestly as you can. Be sure and check only one answer for each question:

## TAKING THE TOXIC ANGER TEST

1. **How often during a typical week does your loved one become angry? (Check one)**

   _____ Not at all

   _____ 1 or 2 times during the week

   _____ 3 to 5 times during the week

   _____ 1 or 2 times each day

   _____ About 3 to 5 times each day

   _____ More than 5 times each day

2. **On average, how intense is your loved one's anger when he/she gets mad? (Circle one)**

   | 1 | 2 | 3 | 4 | 5 | 6 | 7 | 8 | 9 | 10 |
   |---|---|---|---|---|---|---|---|---|---|
   | Mild | | | | | | | | | Extreme |

Now we're going to take your two anger scores and compare them to a large normative group of ordinary men and women, ranging in age from thirteen to eighty, whom we screened for toxic anger at a local health fair some years ago. Interestingly, we found that our survey findings were highly similar to those of Professor James Averill in his intensive study of anger in residents of Greenfield, Massachusetts (population 18,000) and the students of nearby University of Massachusetts.[2]

Take your first score, having to do with how frequently your loved one loses his/her temper, and compare it to the cumulative percentage scores found in Table 1 on the next page. For example, if you said your loved one gets angry "3 to 5 times a day," that would place him or her in the 96th percentile, meaning that they find themselves angry more often than anyone else you might compare them with. Clearly, they are in a small, distinct minority when it comes to anger. On the other hand, if you said your loved one becomes angry only "1 or 2 times a week," this would suggest that, in fact, 50 percent of most other people get angry more frequently than they do, a more mainstream response. The ultimate decision about whether anger is "toxic" then becomes a statistical one—and we have chosen a cutoff point of 84 percent. In effect, when it comes to frequency, toxic anger is anger that is experienced on a *daily* basis, regardless of how strong it is.

*Table 1*
### ANGER FREQUENCY NORMS

| SCORES | CUMULATIVE % |
|---|---|
| Not at all | 11 |
| 1 to 2 times/week | 50 |
| 3 to 5 times/week | 75 |
| 1 to 2 times/day | 84 |
| 3 to 5 times/day | 96 |
| More than 5 times/day | 100 |

Now, repeat the process, comparing the anger intensity score you assigned your loved one to those listed in Table 2 on the next page. Here again, if you said the typical strength of your loved one's anger was a 7, that would suggest that he/she is angrier than 86 percent of our normative group—in other words most people. A rating of only 3, in contrast, would suggest mild anger, a level commonly seen in 27 percent of the general population. Based on this table, anger is toxic when it is experienced at level 7—the 86th percentile—and higher, regardless of how frequently that anger is experienced. How did your loved one fare? Are you surprised by what you found?

*Table 2*

## ANGER INTENSITY NORMS

| SCORES | CUMULATIVE % |
|:------:|:------------:|
| 1 | 8 |
| 2 | 14 |
| 3 | 27 |
| 4 | 42 |
| 5 | 62 |
| 6 | 73 |
| 7 | 86 |
| 8 | 94 |
| 9 | 97 |
| 10 | 100 |

To complete the exercise, let's combine both of these scores to diagnose which sub-type of angry person your loved one fits into and, based on that, whether he/she has *too* much anger. To do this, we are going to consider the first three frequency scores ("Not at all" through "3 to 5 times/week") as representative of infrequent or *episodic* anger, in that the person experiences it on a less than daily basis, which as we can now see is typical of three-fourths of all adolescents and adults. The higher frequency scores ("1 to 2 times/day" through "More than 5 times/day"), we are going to regard as representative of *chronic* anger, occurring repeatedly throughout the day. Similarly, we can subdivide intensity scores into three basic levels: (1–3) *irritability*, (4–6) *mad or angry*, and (7–10) *rage*. This gives a way to objectively classify how angry your loved one is in six possible ways:

|  | *Table 3* | | |
|  | | INTENSITY | |
| FREQUENCY | 1–3 | 4–6 | 7–10 |
| *Less than Daily* | Episodic Irritability | Episodic Anger | Episodic Rage |
| *Daily* | Chronic Irritability | Chronic Anger | Chronic Rage |

## Episodic Irritability

In our normative survey, we find that one-fourth of our respondents (24.8 percent) fall within this category. Such individuals are rarely angered and, even when they are, the intensity of their feelings is extremely mild. Not surprisingly, none of the LBA relationships we described in Chapter One fit this category.

## Episodic Anger

Over a third (35.3 percent) of the people we surveyed describe themselves as getting reasonably angry on an occasional basis. Again, none of the examples in Chapter One describe this level of anger.

## Episodic Rage

Here, we have our first illustration of "toxic" anger. Some 14.7 percent of adolescents and adults in our survey describe themselves (no doubt without meaning to) as episodic ragers. Rage is by far the most intense and dramatic form of anger and the one that leads to the most harm. Five of the seven LBA relationships described in Chapter One involve people who experience episodic rage—Jerry's brother, Sam; Sherri's son; Marilyn's ex-husband; Donald's father; and, Tony's partner, Alan. Their anger wasn't evident every day, but when it was, it was awesome!

## CHRONIC IRRITABILITY

We have found that few people, actually less than 2 percent, fall into this category. Such individuals are often referred to by others as "moody," "hostile," or "bitchy." And while they may not be the most pleasant or attractive people to be around, they are considered harmless and they are unlikely to form the basis for an LBA relationship.

## CHRONIC ANGER

This is the second category of "toxic" anger, typifying 11.2 percent of the people we surveyed. Here, the problem is not the intensity of the person's angry feelings, but rather the fact that they get angry each and every day. Sarah's boyfriend, Todd, provides one such example. You might remember that when asked about his temper, Sarah replied, "we couldn't be in the same room together for more than five minutes without him getting angry at something I was doing." The fact that Todd's anger didn't rise to the level of rage or cause him to act in a violent manner, however, did not make the effect any less traumatic on her. Have no doubt, this is serious anger.

## CHRONIC RAGE

This is the worst-case scenario: the chronic rager. This is the type of person who—like Victor's wife, whose "anger monologues" eventually broke his spirit—experiences extremely intense, out-of-control anger as an everyday part of their LBA relationship. I'm sorry to say that 11.9 percent of those people we surveyed fell into this category.

---

I'll ask again: How did your loved one fare? Do you see what you're up against in this relationship? Now, let's move on to the second crucial question.

# CHAPTER THREE

# WHY ARE THEY SO ANGRY?

Anger is a complex emotion. It is a reaction to a host of diverse factors, including both biological and psychosocial influences. Anger is our nervous system's physical reaction to some threatening perception. No two human beings have the same "recipe" of factors that bring them inevitably to the point of an angry outburst. As such, anger is always an individual, highly personalized experience. To answer the second crucial question, "Why are they so angry?" you need to consider the following:

- Provocation/perceptual styles

- Temperament

- Personality/action tendencies

- Substance use/abuse

- Mood disorders

- Communication problems

- Poor coping skills

- Stress

## Provocation/Perceptual Style

Provocation is perhaps the most overrated explanation of why people get angry. To hear angry people tell it, their emotions are always
provoked by external events and circumstances (triggers): "*That*
made me mad," or "*They* made me hot" or "*She* pushed my but-
tons." In point of fact, however, it is not the things (and people)
that we encounter throughout life that cause us to be irritated, an-
noyed, or enraged, but rather our perceptions and interpretations
of those events and circumstances. For example, two motorists are
sitting at a stoplight, talking on a cell phone while they wait. The
light changes and the driver in the car behind them blows his horn.
One driver waves as if to say "Thank you" for alerting him that it's
time to move forward. The other driver, in sharp contrast, angrily
jumps out of his car and screams, "Who the hell do you think
you're blowing at?" Same situation, but two entirely different reactions. That's the point: *Anger is always a reflection of what's in a
person's mind, not what's going on in the world around him.*

In my earlier book, *Anger-Free,* I talked about four distinct perceptual styles that most often lead people down the path to toxic anger. The first is the *narcissistic* style, in which the person is the "center of their own universe" and fully assumes that everyone around her is there simply to serve and satisfy her unending appetite for recognition, approval, power, and success. Remember Sherri's son? This was the motivating force behind his and most adolescents' episodic rage. Narcissistic individuals can be quite charming and endearing when you give them what they want and feel entitled to, but heaven help you when you don't.

Second, there is the *cynical* style, in which the person begins each day of their life expecting things not to work in their favor and people to, in one way or another, intentionally take advantage of them—and they are ready to react angrily as soon as something happens to prove them right. Sarah's boyfriend, Todd, was cynical, expecting everything she did to be "stupid" and then reacting angrily as if to say, "I knew it!" Cynicism is a self-fulfilling prophecy, to be sure.

Third is the *catastrophic* style, in which the individual reacts with intense emotion (in this case anger, in other cases fear) to any and all frustrations and obstacles they encounter as if they are major, life-threatening events. Minor everyday hassles, which might understandably irritate the rest of us, make these folks furious. In these cases, the anger is always exaggerated. I recall one of my angry clients who recently told me about how he had spent a great deal of time custom-making cabinets for his kitchen, and how when there was one little, correctable problem as he was finishing up the job, he went into a rage, took a crowbar, ripped out all the cabinets and threw them out into the yard. The next day, after he had calmed down, he started the project all over again.

Fourth, there is the *compulsive* style, which, simply stated, reflects an overly serious, "my way or the highway" orientation, wherein the person ends up in an incessant struggle to control every aspect of everyday life—to get everyone else to see and do things his way—only to fail miserably in the end. Marilyn's ex-husband was this type of individual. Years after the divorce, she still remembers vividly how awful it was whenever the two of them tried to work on some task together, like opening and closing the swimming pool each year, and all the abusive anger he directed at her when things didn't go according to his plan. "We just could not do things together," she said. "We would be doing it and everything would be going along fine and then all of a sudden something wasn't fine—I didn't do something his way—and he would just go off."

Does your loved one have a problem with perceptual style?

# Temperament

Temperament describes inherited, inborn traits that basically define the tone or quality of our emotional reactions. Put another way, temperament reflects the way our nervous system is "wired" to respond emotionally to everything from sudden, unexpected noises to anticipated, contentious interpersonal exchanges. Experts agree that up to 50 percent of the emotional side of our personality comes from genes; the rest is a by-product of life experiences. Therein lies the good news: *Even with an angry temperament, it is possible for a person to change.*

There is a continuity to temperament throughout our lives, as they say, "from cradle to the grave."[1] One reason is that people invariably seek out situations and relationships that are compatible with their temperament and thereby avoid any possibility of change. I remember my father had a chance to move from blue-collar work to a white-collar position midway through his life, which would obviously have improved our family's standard of living. But he wasn't happy from the outset because he could not be his angry, confrontational self with his fellow workers. It was not long before he came home and told my mother that he had been demoted back to his old "hands on" job. As strange as it seemed to me at the time, he clearly was relieved, almost happy, at the bad news. The new opportunity simply did not "work" for his temperament. A second reason is that people tend to act in ways that provoke the same counterreactions in others, which in turn reinforces their temperamental style. Thus, angry people tend to provoke anger in others, including loved ones, which give them even more reason and justification for continuing their anger.

Two temperamental traits that definitely appear associated with toxic anger are *impulsivity* and *excitability*. Impulsivity refers to an individual's inability to delay gratification or tolerate frustration (and the tension that goes with it) when his needs are not immediately satisfied. Excitability, on the other hand, has to do with the vigor or "explosiveness" of one's emotions. Some people are never just happy; they're ecstatic. They are never just blue, but extremely distraught. They are never just concerned when things go wrong, they panic. Both of these traits, I have found, tend to be most strongly linked to the intensity—moreso than frequency—of a person's anger, e.g., leading to rage in situations where others only seem to get irritated.

Does your loved one have a problem with temperament?

## Personality/Action Tendencies

Strangely enough, almost nothing is known about the role that personality plays in predisposing people to excessive, toxic anger. Psychologists have long studied various aspects of human personality—agreeableness, shyness, extraversion, optimism—but, unfortunately, have not directly linked such traits to the likelihood of a person becoming *too* angry.

One exception is that of the "aggressive" personality. In this context, aggressive refers to the type of person who naturally and easily takes charge, initiates change, and makes things happen in everyday life—as distinct, say, from shy, passive, or dependent personalities. Let's not confuse being aggressive with aggression, the latter characterizing actions intended to hurt, harm, or destroy people and things. The aggressive personality may or may not exhibit aggression. What I'm really talking about are people who actively pursue what they want and move forward with determination.

The concept of an aggressive personality embodies a number of sub-traits or specific action-tendencies—consistent, predictable, visible patterns of interaction with one's environment across a wide variety of situations and settings and over long periods of time. These various traits/tendencies are summarized in the following test, which was developed solely for the purpose of predicting a person's potential for maladaptive anger. Take a minute and complete the test, answering each of the ten questions in terms of how you would best describe the person with whom you currently share an LBA relationship.

---

## THE AGGRESSIVE PERSONALITY QUESTIONNAIRE

*(Check one answer for each question)*

1. My loved one is _____ competitive person.

   ___ (1) not a                  ___ (2) a somewhat

   ___ (3) a fairly               ___ (4) a moderately

   ___ (5) a very

2. Others see my loved one as a forceful person when he/she is pursuing a goal.

   ___ (1) not really             ___ (2) somewhat

   ___ (3) probably               ___ (4) definitely

   ___ (5) absolutely

3. In working on a task, my loved one tends to be _____ persistent.

   ____ (1) not very           ____ (2) a little

   ____ (3) fairly               ____ (4) moderately

   ____ (5) very

4. In a situation involving conflict, my loved one is _____ confrontational.

   ____ (1) not              ____ (2) somewhat

   ____ (3) fairly            ____ (4) definitely

   ____ (5) extremely

5. My family and friends would say my loved one is an impatient person.

   ____ (1) not really         ____ (2) maybe a little

   ____ (3) probably          ____ (4) definitely

   ____ (5) absolutely

6. At times, my loved one can be a demanding person.

   ____ (1) no               ____ (2) a little

   ____ (3) sure             ____ (4) definitely

   ____ (5) absolutely

7. My friends view my loved one as an intense person.

   ____ (1) not really         ____ (2) maybe a little

   ____ (3) probably          ____ (4) sure

   ____ (5) definitely

8. My loved one is a _____ determined person if he/she wants something.

_____ (1) not very  _____ (2) fairly

_____ (3) somewhat  _____ (4) moderately

_____ (5) very

9. In dealing with others, my loved one tends to be _____ direct.

_____ (1) not very  _____ (2) a little

_____ (3) fairly  _____ (4) pretty

_____ (5) very

10. I believe it is fair to say that my loved one is a dominant person when it comes to social relationships.

_____ (1) I don't think so  _____ (2) not sure

_____ (3) maybe a little  _____ (4) pretty much

_____ (5) absolutely

Now, add up your numbers (values assigned to each of your answers in parentheses) to determine how likely it is that you are in an LBA relationship with someone who has an aggressive personality. APQ Score: _____

Scores range from 10 to 50 with higher scores indicating a more aggressive personality. Scores between 10 and 20 essentially describe a nonaggressive person. (You'll have to look elsewhere for the explanation of their anger!) Scores between 21 and 35 reflect an average degree of aggressiveness. And scores between 36 and 50 suggest a highly aggressive personality. How did your loved one fare?

Our research has shown that APQ scores are linked to how often someone loses their temper as well as the intensity of their anger. Low APQ scorers, for example, typically get mad once or twice a week (episodic), as contrasted with high scorers, who report episodes of anger at least once or twice each day (chronic). Similarly, high APQ scorers, most often report experiencing "rage" compared to low scorers who more often described feeling only "irritated." High APQ scores are also highly correlated with the Type A (coronary-prone) personality.

While those of us who spend much of our life in an aggressive pursuit of our life-goals are thus more likely to have a bad temper, clearly not all aspects of an aggressive personality are bad. Many Americans, for example, actively seek out the services of an aggressive stockbroker; hire an aggressive attorney to defend them in court; welcome what they perceive to be an aggressive approach to some life-threatening illness; and champion the most aggressive athletes at all levels of sport. Is this bad? Certainly not. In fact, further analysis of the relationship of the APQ to one's propensity for anger suggests that it may be only a subset of these aggressive traits (items 4, 5, 6, 7, and 10 in the quiz)—confrontational, impatient, demanding, intense, and dominant—that predispose people to toxic anger. Being competitive, forceful in pursuing goals, persistent, determined, and direct may have little to do with losing one's temper and may, in fact, be seen as highly desirable features of the person whom you love. Many of you may actually have been attracted to this person for this "good" side of their aggressive personality (competitive, forceful), only to discover later they also had the "bad" side (confrontational, demanding).

## Substance Use/Abuse

Abusive anger and aggressive exchange between partners in an LBA relationship frequently occur within the context of drug use and abuse. A host of chemical substances, both legal and illegal, act on the human brain in ways that can, and often do, result in impaired reasoning and judgment, belligerence, and exacerbated emotion, particularly anger. The American Psychiatric Association's Diagnostic and Statistical Manual for Mental Disorders, for example, lists anger-related symptomatology for all of the following types of drug abuse and dependence: alcohol; cocaine; chemical inhalants (cleaning fluids); phencyclidine (PCP); and sedative, hypnotic, and anxiolytic drugs. Research has shown that anti-anxiety drugs such as Valium can lead to noticeably increased irritability and aggression,[2] thus substituting one emotional problem for another. Even more commonly used substances such as caffeine[3] and nicotine[4] can act to stimulate, rather than "tranquilize," the nervous system, resulting in a heightened disposition toward negative emotion—nervousness, depression, and anger. And last, but not least, is the link between anabolic steroid use and abusive anger,[5] especially among athletes.

Of these, without doubt, the overuse of alcohol is the biggest contributor to toxic anger. Why? Because the public use of alcohol is second only to that of caffeine and it has a much more potent effect. Alcohol—even though most of us use it as a means of temporary escape from the rigors of everyday life—stimulates our nervous system, causing us to become more aroused and emotionally reactive, not less. Talk about a paradox! We start out trying to "mellow out" and end up ranting and raving.

Other links between anger and alcohol include:

- One out of three men who consume alcohol is an "angry drinker" who predictably loses his temper every time he gets intoxicated.[6]

- This number increases to 54 percent for high-quantity drinkers.

- Angry drinkers have more hangover symptoms than non-angry drinkers.

- Alcohol consumption leads to heightened misperception of anger in others and a readiness to react aggressively.[7]

- Women who are moderate/heavy drinkers are more apt to lose their temper than are women who are non-/light drinkers.[8]

- Women who drink excessively are more likely to experience anger when sober than women who drink less.

- Women who give up drinking experience a significant decrease in anger as compared to those who continue to use alcohol.

Does your loved one have a substance abuse problem?

## Mood Disorders

Psychiatrist John Ratey and his co-author Dr. Catherine Johnson, in their excellent book *Shadow Syndromes,* conclude: "Depressed people are all too frequently angry people as well, certainly irritable if nothing else." They go on to explain that what they call "anger attacks" (episodic rage in our terminology) result much more than one might expect from underlying mood disorders. The primary culprit here seems to be depression, even in its mildest (albeit chronic) form—dysthymia. There appears to be a chemical imbalance involving brain neurotransmitters—epinephrine and serotonin—in depressed folks that lead to increased feelings of anger. Those who suffer from a *retarded* depression (what Freud called melancholia) tend to suppress their anger, while those suffering from an *agitated* mood disorder express it all too readily through sudden emotional outbursts. Interestingly, Ratey and Johnson further argue that, for at least some depressed people, "anger can bring sluggish areas in the brain up to speed," suggesting that anger may unwittingly be a way of self-medicating a chronic mood disturbance. I can certainly agree with their assessment of the interplay between toxic anger and depression, based on my three decades of treating countless patients who exhibit both types of symptoms. As one rather depressed-sounding woman who was attending one of my anger workshops put it, "Anger is one way I know I'm alive." One can only imagine how she feels when she is not mad at someone or something.

Further, research has demonstrated that antidepressant drugs can virtually eliminate rage in the vast majority of those treated and the beneficial effects begin to emerge almost immediately, thus also linking depression to anger.

Does your loved one suffer from depression?

## Communication Problems

Angry people are communicating something with their emotion—the question is, what? Emotions remain one of the most common forms of nonverbal communication among humans. They represent a continuing link to our animal past, a time before we had developed the spoken language. Each emotion tells its own story. Sadness is about loss, fear communicates a sense of vulnerability, and pain tells the world that we are injured and need help.

Anger typically has been regarded as the emotion of both commitment and protest. Anger communicates what it is that we are most committed to in life, what we value. Anger in adolescents, like Sherri's son, usually reflects an abiding, rather exclusive commitment to self—in other words, "The only thing that is important here is **me** and what I want!" The type of anger that causes people to write letters to the editor of a newspaper more often represents the commitment one has to principles involving the rights of others and issues such as fairness, truth, and personal responsibility. Anger can also be an accusation or protest against some perceived misdeed. Tony's partner, Alan, flew into a rage when Tony put the mail in the wrong place. Was that really the misdeed or was Alan angry because, as he saw it, Tony was violating **his** space, **his** territory, and threatening to take over **his** world? We don't know—and that's the problem with using emotions to communicate important issues in life. And we can't know unless Alan tells us in his own words. Bottom line: *Anger is a form of communication to be sure, but a very poor form indeed!*

Relationship anger may also communicate other negative feelings such as contempt and disgust. The angry partner in an LBA relationship often treats his/her loved one as someone who is vile and worthless, someone to be disrespected and despised. Similarly, the accompanying feeling of disgust signals that the loved one is viewed as repulsive and someone with whom no pleasure can be derived. In interpersonal terms, both of these emotions share an element of social rejection, signaling that the other person is not worthy of our affection or attention. Psychologist John Gottman, a leading expert on the dynamics of dysfunctional marriages, believes that contempt—which he sees as the primary cause of failed relationships—goes far beyond ordinary criticism in that its intent is to insult, demean, and psychologically abuse the partner.[9] It is my belief that when this emotional triad of anger-contempt-disgust is evident in a relationship, there is a heightened risk of physical violence.

What is your loved one communicating with his/her anger?

## Poor Coping Skills

For many people, anger is a way—sometimes the only way they know—of coping with the challenges, conflicts, and pitfalls of everyday life. The best example I know to illustrate that fact has to do with my parents, both of whom I love, but neither of whom were skilled at problem solving. I still remember vividly the time when I was about ten years old and I accidentally shut a door on my baby brother's finger. My mother and some neighbors rushed him to the hospital emergency room, where doctors saved his finger, and at the same time called my father at work to let him know what had happened. My father, instead of going to the hospital to see about my brother, instead came home where, in an obvious state of rage, he single-handedly removed every door from our house—front door, back door, bedroom doors, bathroom door, closet doors—and with a vengeance threw each one out into the yard. This was my father's way of coping with the possibility of one of his children losing a finger in an accident. Meanwhile, my favorite aunt, knowing my father's temper, had spirited me away lest he "dismantle" me as well! Such scenes, while dramatic, were not uncommon in my family, where all problems, large or small, were dealt with by my parents in the same way—they just got angry. I recall thinking, even as a child: *Surely, there's a better way!*

Why do some people lack adequate coping skills and instead have to rely on anger as a way of dealing with stress? Because they are not taught these skills early in life. Sadly enough, many families spend more time teaching youngsters how to play tennis or do algebra than they do teaching them, both by instruction and modeling, how to problem-solve in everyday life. Worse yet, far too many provide examples of poor coping, which are then handed down from one generation to another. One man whom I evaluated for child abuse, in fact, defended his abusive behavior, suggesting that he was only disciplining his son the way his father had disciplined him—with severe physical punishment. And he was not about to let me or anyone else tell him that his father, whom he loved, was wrong.

Daniel Goleman, author of the best-selling book, *Emotional Intelligence,* states rather emphatically that "One of the most essential emotional lessons, first learned in infancy and refined throughout childhood, is how to soothe oneself when upset." Parents who are effective at "emotional coaching" help their children to distinguish between intensities of emotion—irritability versus rage—and view their child's anger as a teachable moment. Rather than simply dismiss or criticize their child's anger, instead they help the youngster label the feeling appropriately, identify the causes for their anger, distinguish between feelings (anger) and actions (aggression), and, most importantly, problem-solve.[10] Those children fortunate enough to have such coaching rarely experience toxic anger.

Can your loved one cope effectively with his/her problems or does he/she just get mad?

## Stress

There is no such thing as a stress-free life. All human beings are confronted with challenges, crises, and conflicts every day. Whether stress turns into anger, however, depends on the amount and type of stress each person must deal with at any given time. Each of us has a certain "carrying capacity" or tolerance for stress, i.e., how much our nervous system can handle without showing signs of emotional strain. That's what anger is—a type of emotional strain. When stress mounts up and exceeds our stress capacity, that's when we are most apt to lose our temper. A small amount of "excess" stress typically manifests itself as irritability, a larger excess as full-blown anger or rage. Individual variations in stress tolerance may be due to genetic differences in "stress reactivity," how people are raised, and other mediating factors such as social support, personality hardiness, and a sense of self-efficacy, all of which I will discuss later in this book. Some people believe that the more stress you are exposed to, the more you learn to deal with it. Nothing could be further from the truth. My parents certainly had no shortage of stress in their lives, but they never learned how to deal with it other than to be angry. That is one of the reasons I have long since forgiven them for their toxic anger. As bad as it was at times, they did the best they knew how.

The type of stress also makes a difference, though not in the way you might expect. Odd as it may seem, it is the minor stresses (hassles)—hurrying to complete a task, being ignored by others, car trouble—that mostly affect our emotional state, not the major ones like divorce, death, or loss of a job.[11] Why is that? Three simple reasons: (1) they occur much more often—while we have loved ones die only every so often, we can run into troublesome neighbors every day; (2) we tend to trivialize the impact of minor stresses and thus passively accept and absorb them rather than dealing with them in a more proactive, direct fashion; and, (3) we are more likely to deal with hassles by ourselves, without asking for help from supportive others as we are more likely to do when we are confronted with major stresses. Stresses that accumulate over time, ones that are chronic, and ones that seem beyond our control, are also much more likely to lead to anger.

Is your loved one suffering from stress overload?

————

I have expressly chosen not to focus on anger that is sometimes symptomatic of certain physical diseases and disorders such as that found in some individuals who have suffered a stroke that affects the "emotional systems" of the brain, those who are afflicted with an Attention Deficit/Hyperactivity Disorder in which there is a component of impulsivity, those suffering from chronic pain disorders, and those with certain forms of epilepsy. My experience in treating angry people and their loved ones over the years has taught me that these latter groups actually account for only a small number of LBA relationships.

Having read through all the various reasons why people tend to be *too* angry, you may now want to return to pages 37–38 and put a check mark next to each of those factors which you believe contribute to your loved one's anger. This will give you some idea of exactly how big his/her problem is and will also help you appreciate my answers to the remaining two questions: When will their anger stop? and What can I do to stop them from being so angry?

# CHAPTER FOUR

# STOP THE ANGER

What most readers really want to know is, when will my loved one's anger stop? Can toxic anger be cured? What can I do to make him/her less angry? These are legitimate questions and ones that must be answered definitively before you can be convinced that embarking on the seven-step recovery program that follows is something you really want to commit yourself to.

As to whether toxic anger can be cured, consider the following: There is some evidence in our survey studies that toxic anger tends to subside with age. That's the good news. Over twice as many of our respondents who were under age forty reported problematic anger (48.6 percent) as compared to those over forty years old (21.2 percent). When we look at the self-reported frequency and intensity of anger decade by decade, beginning in the teenage years and up through people sixty-plus years of age, we note a steady decline in the average anger experience for each group beginning around age thirty. Why is that? Some have suggested that as people grow older, they appear to be less impulsive, to have less intense physiological arousal associated with anger, and to gain more internal (self) control over their negative feelings.[1] Older people also tend to be more selective with whom they interact, avoiding people who might otherwise provoke them.

So, what's the bad news? The bad news is that this "mellowing out" process does not have a noticeable effect until, at best, the second half of life, sometime after age forty. And, even then, our findings show that one out of six forty- to eighty-years-olds are still reporting at least episodic rage. To make matters worse, we also know that men are less likely than women to show this age-related decline in toxic anger, and men remain the most likely "dispensers" of anger in LBA relationships.

At this point, you are probably feeling rather discouraged, right? Don't be—there is some hope! Anger management of the type I offered in my book *Anger-Free,* as it turns out, does help people detoxify their anger and does so in a reasonably short period of time. For example, those folks who participate in our ten-week anger classes typically report an overall decrease of 32 percent in how often they get angry and a drop of 51 percent in the intensity of their anger. Our clients start out being angry three to five times a week and end up, ten weeks later, feeling angry only one or two times a week. The intensity of their anger, on the whole, decreases from 5.54 (mad) to 2.71 (irritable). The majority of our graduates (70 percent) continue to report success in controlling their tempers months after the program as well. Needless to say, I am quite encouraged by these statistics.

With that in mind, the question arises: Why don't more people with anger problems seek the cure? More to the point, why do you think your loved one hasn't yet found a way to stop his/her abusive anger? There are several possible answers to this question: First, it is conceivable that your loved one actually does not know they have a problem. Samuel Clemens ("Mark Twain"), for example, was quoted as saying, "A thunder stroke fell upon me out of the most unsuspected of skies. I found that, all their lives, my children had been afraid of me, had stood all their days in uneasy dread of my sharp tongue and uncertain temper . . . And I never suspected." This is why, as I suggest in Chapter Eleven, "silence is not golden" when it comes to dealing with other people's anger.

Second, it is possible, even likely, that your loved one knows they have a problem, but that problem, as they see it, is you. You are the one provoking them, getting on their nerves, frustrating them, and basically keeping them from getting whatever it is that they feel entitled to in life. You, not they, are both the cause of and the solution to their anger. So, it makes sense that you are the one that needs to change, not them.

Third, your loved one may, in fact, have a positive incentive to continue his/her angry ways. A young man attended one of our anger management classes some years ago, complaining that he had been forced to get help by his wife who was tired of putting up with his temper and also by his employer who had sanctioned him several times because of angry outbursts on the job. One would think that he would be motivated to change, right? To the contrary, in the third meeting, he proudly announced to the other participants in the group that he "enjoyed" having a bad temper—he felt physically powerful when he became angry and he liked the feeling of intimidating others. Anger was clearly fueling his aggressive—intense, dominant, confrontational—personality. I suggested that it would probably be difficult for him to give up such behavior since he found pleasure in it. He agreed, and he never returned for the remaining seven classes. Ironically, several months later, he called back saying that he was now separated and had lost his job because of his anger, and he thought maybe it was time to make a change. I scheduled him for an appointment a few days later, but he never showed up. The biggest obstacle I find in trying to help adolescents let go of toxic anger is that they are getting something positive out of it: it empowers them to stand up to bullies, distracts them from the normal social anxieties that all adolescents at that age have, and is a wonderful way of controlling their parents, who will often do anything just to appease their temper.

Fourth, your loved one may well not appreciate the complex nature of toxic anger. As we saw in Chapter Three, there is no single or simple answer to, "Why are they so angry?" Even motivated clients often fail to curb their temper because they do not address enough of the root causes to see any evidence of improvement. This is why angry people need professional help and why they need a comprehensive program of anger management that goes beyond simply counting to ten when you find yourself getting mad or taking a few deep breaths to calm yourself down. Try doing that when you're in a full-blown state of rage and see what happens.

Fifth, your loved one may not accept responsibility for seeking an anger cure, because you have, at least in the past, too readily accepted that responsibility for him/her. Most of the calls I get for anger management, for example, are made not by the person who needs help, but by their parents, spouses, and family. Many of the *Anger-Free* books I sell are, again, not to angry people, but rather to their girlfriends, wives, and mothers. Such efforts, while well intended, are, as I point out later in this book, part of an enabling process that fosters the continuation of toxic anger in those you love.

Lastly—and this is really not your loved one's fault—there is quite honestly a dearth of mental health professionals who are interested in or adequately trained to assist people who suffer from the Toxic Anger Syndrome. Part of the problem stems from the fact that the profession of psychiatry has yet to formally acknowledge emotional disorders of anger in the same way they have disorders of anxiety and depression. And because of this, health insurance companies typically do not provide resources to cover such treatment. One hopes all this will change in the foreseeable future.

So, where does that leave you? Is there nothing you can do to help your loved one stop the anger? Actually, there is. You can read this book in its entirety, complete all seven steps necessary for recovery from damage inflicted by the LBA relationship, and in so doing eliminate many of the barriers your loved one has to overcome if he/she is to get the help he/she needs. If you commit yourself to the principles outlined this book, your loved one will no longer be able to ignore the problem he/she has with anger, he/she will no longer be able to use you as an excuse for his/her outrageous behavior, and he/she will have to accept responsibility for making a change. In other words, you can help your loved one best by beginning to help yourself. Instead of waiting for him/her to change, don't you think it is time you take the lead? You can begin this process by first assessing the many ways you have been hurt because you happened to love an angry person.

# CHAPTER FIVE

# DAMAGE ASSESSMENT

Toxic anger can be hazardous to your health and safety. A loving but angry relationship can damage everything from a person's physical and emotional health to his/her social, occupational, and economic well-being. Some damage is obvious and visible for all to see, but most is not. Only one of the seven "stories" highlighted in Chapter One, for example, involved actual physical violence. For the other six victims, there were, as Marilyn said, "no bruises or broken bones."

The following account illustrates the detrimental impact of abusive anger on others: I had been treating chronic pain patients for over thirty years. So, quite naturally, I thought I knew everything there was to know about the various factors that exacerbate pain, in effect "making a bad situation worse": excessive use of narcotics; sedentary lifestyle; depression; lack of support from family and friends. But I was wrong. There was one pain-enhancing factor that had until recently escaped my attention, and that was toxic anger.

In fact, I have found that 72 percent of my pain clients suffer from excessive anger.

A couple of years ago, I was in the process of conducting a five-week rehabilitation class with a small group of chronic pain patients when one morning, as we went around the table recapping the activities of the previous day, one of the participants suddenly jumped up and embarked on a tirade that ended up lasting almost an hour. Along the way, he was joined by the other three patients until all four were simultaneously venting their rage, all directed squarely at me. Not wanting to appear unduly defensive and eager to allow the patients to unburden themselves emotionally, I sat passively throughout, saying nothing. I was "cool," unruffled, I thought, by their venomous accusations.

Eventually, the group exhausted itself, things got quiet, and we proceeded on cautiously with the morning's formal agenda. Three hours later, they left for the day. And then it happened. As I went to get up from the table—just minutes after the last client drove away—I felt an excruciating pain in my lower back that literally dropped me to my knees. The pain was so intense I couldn't get up from the floor for at least ten minutes and then it was all I could do to walk (actually hobble) next door to my office, where I was forced to cancel the remainder of my day.

At home, lying in bed, I thought about what might have caused my back to suddenly go into such severe spasm. I had not lifted anything or injured myself in any way. What had happened was that my whole body had instinctively, automatically, and without any conscious effort on my part gone into a defensive posture that matched the clients' anger in intensity. This, in turn, had produced a state of hypertension in my lower back muscles, which is my "Achilles' heel" because of a sedentary lifestyle and previous history of back injury. The intense, collective rage of those four people had, in effect, thrown my back out—that's how their anger hurt me.

The next morning, I shared my insight with the group—all of whom were subdued following the previous day's outburst—and concluded by saying to them, "If your anger can do that to my back, think what it must be doing to yours." These four very angry people were speechless. Dr. John E. Sarno, author of *Mind Over Back Pain,* believes that this connection between anger-tension-pain, what he calls the "tension myositis syndrome" is responsible for the vast majority of chronic pain disorders thought to be caused by abnormalities of the spine such as herniated discs and pinched nerves.

The toxic effects of anger are analogous to those of passive smoking. We know that nonsmokers who constantly inhale other people's cigarette smoke suffer immediately in terms of eye irritation, cough, headaches, sore throat, and nausea and, over a lifetime, have a 25 percent increased risk for both heart disease and lung cancer, even though they themselves never smoke. The evidence is so strong that secondhand smoke is now considered to play a "causative" role in both of these potentially lethal diseases.

I would argue that the same is true for those of you who are overexposed to "secondhand anger." The risks associated with excessive anger can, I suggest, all too often be shared by both parties in an LBA relationship. What are those risks? We know, for example, that "high anger" men are three times more likely to have a heart attack—even after other traditional risk factors such as family history, blood pressure, cholesterol, and weight are taken into account—

than "low anger" males.[1] Our own research has shown that highly angry men and women are much more likely to be "at risk" for coronary disease because they are more apt to consume excessive amounts of alcohol (two-plus drinks at a sitting), smoke cigarettes, report a significant loss of energy and vitality, and feel overworked. I think it is highly probable that the health risk of loved ones on the receiving end of such anger is also substantial. The "defensiveness" I experienced in dealing with those rageful pain patients could just as easily manifest itself in cardiac symptoms in those vulnerable to cardiovascular disease by family history, for example.

And what about the indirect impact of secondhand anger in terms of social and economic consequences? If Jerry, the young man I featured in Chapter One, had died of a heart attack, his young widow would have been left with few financial resources with which to raise two children. Spouses and families of angry people are also adversely affected because, as we now know, their angry loved one is much more likely to terminate his/her education early, work at lower paying jobs, and have less stable employment over a lifetime, and the marriage is twice as likely to end in divorce.

Who's hurt most by toxic anger, the person who is angry or those closest to him/her? It's hard to say. Let's look at some other examples of lives damaged by anger.

## The High Cost of Intimate Partner Violence

A parent's worst fear is that harm will come to his/her children. Unfortunately, parents may be totally unaware of one type of harm that is occurring with alarming frequency, especially among their daughters: *Intimate Partner Violence (IPV)*. This type of LBA relationship is epidemic among girls of high-school age. One in five, in fact, experience IPV before they graduate and move on to an adult world.[2] What is IPV? According to a recent article published in the *Journal of the American Medical Association*, it is any act that results in a young woman being "hurt physically or sexually by a date or someone they were going with"—acts motivated in most instances by toxic anger.

Interestingly, IPV does not appear isolated to any particular subset of adolescent females, for example, those seen as somehow being disadvantaged by socioeconomic circumstances. To the contrary, a small study I conducted among thirty high-school senior girls competing in a national scholarship program revealed that 40 percent had already been in a loving relationship with someone who was very angry, 23 percent were still in a relationship with someone who had a bad temper, 27 percent had been hurt physically (shoved, slapped, hit) by someone they were dating, 53 percent had been subjected to verbal abuse from someone they loved, and, 57 percent knew a peer who was also in an LBA relationship. And these young women were the best and brightest in their respective schools, the ones with the most talents and resources, from "good" homes with lots of family support, the ones most likely to succeed—and the ones who you might think would be smart enough to recognize a dangerous relationship when they saw it. But, then again, as they say, love is blind!

What sort of damage did IPV inflict on these young women? The results of the aforementioned study of over four thousand girls suggests that it led to a host of self-destructive behaviors: heavy smoking, binge drinking, driving after drinking, cocaine use, unhealthy weight control (diet pills, laxative use), early (before age fifteen) and unsafe (not using a condom, multiple partners) sex, unplanned pregnancy, and, a heightened potential for suicide. Could it get any worse? These young women had not only learned to be victims within the context of an LBA relationship, they had also learned all too well how to victimize themselves.

Do you have a son or daughter who suffers from IPV?

## Daddy Dearest

The most damaging LBA relationships we humans have are those we experience at the earliest stage of life—with our parents. Anne, a sixty-two-year-old recently retired office manager, illustrates just how lasting and emotionally "crippling" the effects of such a relationship can be:

Anne's father was a "difficult, always difficult" man. In fact, he was a chronic rager, who was angry every day of her life while she was growing up.

"He would yell, scream, and throw things," she remembers "and be completely disgusted by everything we did." He was extremely narcissistic—"our whole lives centered around him"—and someone who demanded absolute perfection in all things. "If we got an A, he wanted to know why we didn't get an A+. You never did it right enough."

Did Anne love her father? "When I was a child, I adored him. I thought he was the handsomest and smartest man in the world." Did she love him until he died? "No. He was such a jerk. I just got to where I couldn't stand him. Late in life, he apologized, but it was too late." Anne only saw her father twice during the last five years of his life, which were spent in a nursing home.

How did this love-anger relationship with her father affect her? It made her life an unending psychological struggle, one beset by problems with self-esteem, a lack of identity, suppressed emotions, a feeling of being ill at ease around others, and, worst of all, a sense of "utter self-loathing." "Even now," she explains, "if I had to describe myself, I wouldn't know what to say. I wouldn't have a clue other than what I was wearing." One of the survival instincts Anne learned early on to deal with her father's rage, you see, was to become invisible: "My sister would fight back, but I'd be really quiet and hope I could get out of the room without him noticing—and I still do that." Anne had learned to be invisible even from herself.

Anne has never felt like she was important, valued for who she is or anything she does. One of the things she dislikes about herself— and there are many—is the fact that she constantly finds herself "hoping people will tell me what a good job I've done, even over silly, routine things" that really don't deserve recognition.

Anne is also her own worst critic, observing and judging everything she says and does, lest she risk being seen by others as "stupid." "It's crazy. I even rehearse conversations I'm going to have with other people before they happen to make sure I express myself the right way. Believe me, I can feel foolish just saying hi."

All her life, she has "put up with accusations from people without ever once questioning whether they were true. I figure I must have done something to make them feel that way." Only in recent years has she started to think, "Maybe the problem isn't with me; maybe it's with them." That itself has been a liberating experience.

And lastly, Anne has always thought of herself—unlike her father—as someone who doesn't get angry. It was only at age forty-eight, when she found herself becoming furious when "little things didn't go right" and actually remembers "seeing my father's face when I felt like lashing out," that she realized for the first time she, too, was capable of experiencing toxic anger. In effect, she had become her father's daughter after all. To this day, Anne finds herself waking up in the middle of the night "just furious. It's like I wake up and don't have time to get my guard up," a guard she has used quite effectively to keep people out and her emotions in.

And the most amazing thing of all: her father managed to create all this damage without ever laying a hand on her. "Not once do I remember him hitting us."

Have you ever had an LBA relationship that left you feeling like Anne?

## A Dampening Effect

One of the more subtle yet far-reaching effects of an LBA relationship is that it serves to "dampen" the more positive aspects of one's personality: joy, spontaneity, generosity, freedom to express one's thoughts and feelings openly, and love. The following is an illustration:

I was sitting in a local restaurant one mornir̶
breakfast. I was seated in a booth next to a fam
and their teenage daughter. When I arrived, the motn̶
ter were engaged in active conversation with each other and ṳ̶
ther, and they appeared excited about whatever it was they were
talking about. You got the sense that this was, for this family, the
beginning of what would turn out to be a happy day all around.
Then, all of a sudden, the father put a damper on the whole situation. He had obviously become irritated at something that was said
and, as he spoke in a quiet but hostile tone, he appeared to get even
angrier. All conversation except by him ceased and the mother and
daughter never spoke again for the remainder of the meal. Their
faces lost all appearance of joy and there was no further eye contact
between any of the three. All the enthusiasm that had been apparent vanished, and all that remained was an alienated group of
"strangers." When the man went to pay the check, I noticed the
woman hug her child, standing there silent and sad as if all life had
been taken out of them.

Such scenes have a particularly disturbing effect on me because
this is exactly the sort of family I grew up in. And, because of that,
to this day at sixty years of age, I find it difficult to enjoy life as
many of my close friends and family do. I'm too cautious about
sharing my more intimate feelings; I rarely take "risks"—stock
market, business ventures, initiating new relationships, or for that
matter hang-gliding in Hawaii with my children; I worry about far
too many little things; I'm way too serious; and, even though I am
good at making other people laugh, I rarely laugh myself. For me,
this is the enduring effect of having LBA relationships early in life

and the thing I find most difficult to forgive. There are moments when I grieve for a life never lived.

## Third-Party Damage

One can be harmed by LBA relationships to which they are not even a party. Take, for instance, Alex, a thirty-three-year-old man who came seeking counseling but, when asked, wasn't sure exactly what his problem was. He had a good job, a new car, by all accounts a beautiful fiancée, a solid stock portfolio, was well on his way to owning his own home—the good life—yet he was miserable, rather dispirited, and lacking in gusto. He wanted me to help him figure out why.

On his fifth visit, I found the answer: I was talking with Alex about his childhood and I asked him what happened when his parents became angry. He thought a minute and replied, "Oh, my parents never got angry." I was astonished! I asked him how old he was when he finally left home to be on his own and he said twenty. "In all those twenty years, you never once saw your parents angry?" I asked again. "No. Not once" was his answer. Before I could go on, however, he volunteered, "Now there were many occasions when they wouldn't speak to one another for long periods of time—days, weeks even—but I don't recall them ever being angry." And why did he think, either as a child or a young man, that these two people would go so long without speaking? He didn't know.

I explained to Alex that his parents apparently had such an angry relationship that they literally could not speak—that's how powerful their negative feelings for each other were. And that was also why he had grown up learning to have no emotions, a condition psychiatrists call alexithymia, which left him feeling chronically alienated, unable to form intimate attachments, depressed, and generally miserable. Not only did Alex not know when he was angry, he didn't know when he was happy, sad, frustrated, lonely, content, or scared. The damage he suffered as a by-product of his parents' LBA relationship was not from what they did to him, but rather from what they didn't do for him—they didn't teach him to feel.

Have you suffered any third-party damage?

**Below, list all the ways you believe your loved one's anger has affected your life:**

**PHYSICAL**

1. *My boyfriend has physically assaulted me on more than one occasion.*

2. _____

3. _____

4. _____

**EMOTIONAL**

1. *I am in counseling for depression as a result of my mother's rage.*

2. _____

3. _____

4. _____

**SOCIAL**

1. *I have lost several good friends because of my wife's anger.* _____

2. _____

3. _____

4. _____

**RELATIONSHIP**

1. *My brother got mad at me a year ago and I haven't seen him since.*

2. _____

3. _____

4. _____

**ENERGY**

1. *I never feel fresh and rested when I wake up in the morning.* _____

2. _____

3. _____

4. _____

**SUBSTANCE USE**

1. *After one of my father's outbursts, I have to have a drink.* _____

2. _____

3. _____

4. _____

**OCCUPATIONAL**

1. *After one of my son's tantrums, I have trouble concentrating at work.*

2. _____

3. _____

4. _____

**ECONOMIC**

1. *My husband is out of work now because of his temper.*

2. _____

3. _____

4. _____

**LEGAL**

1. *I had to get a restraining order against my son because of his violence.*

2. _____

3. _____

4. _____

Now that you have assessed the damage, are you ready to make a change?

# CHAPTER SIX

# IS IT POSSIBLE TO CHANGE?

As I suggested in Chapter Four, the best way you can help your loved one stop the anger and at the same time repair the damage already inflicted on you by this relationship is to redirect your energies into a program of self-change, which will be outlined in the chapters that follow. Before proceeding, however, you need to address the issues such as:

- What are your intentions regarding self-change?

- How capable are you when it comes to self-change?

- What do you have to look forward to if you change?

- How "hardy" are you?

- How resigned are you to being a victim of someone else's anger?

# Are You Ready for Change?

There is probably no human being alive who does not want to change something about themselves. Millions of Americans say they *want* to quit smoking. Millions more *want* to lose weight. Still others *want* to cut back on their use of alcohol, *want* to improve their health through regular exercise, *want* to pay off accumulated debt, *want* to spend more quality time with their kids, *want* more time to relax—and I could go on and on. But alas, the vast majority will never achieve any of these worthy goals. Why not? Simple: they're not ready to commit themselves to a process of change, to do the hard work that is required to realize meaningful change in their lives. In other words, *wanting is not enough—you have to be ready to change.*

Over a decade ago, Drs. James Prochaska and Carlo Di-Clemente introduced the concept of "psychological readiness"[1] to the field of behavioral psychology and they and their colleagues have since applied it to a wide variety of changes in healthy (exercise, cancer screening) and unhealthy (alcohol, smoking, obesity, opiate use) behavior. Basically, they argue that intention leads to change and that people differ tremendously in how *intentional* (or ready) they are for change. Prochaska and DiClemente propose five stages of readiness, which essentially describe the starting point for a person's effort to change some aspect of his/her behavior, in this case, being a victim of someone else's anger. They refer to the first stage as the *no intention* stage—the person is not aware that a change needs to be made. This type of individual might even become irritated when a friend or family member mentions their loved one's outrageous behavior. The second stage is the *preintention* stage, in which the person begins to consider, but not yet act on, the possibility that they are in an LBA relationship which is hurting them. Such individuals might browse through the self-improvement section of a local bookstore for books like this one. They are weighing the pros and cons of taking some type of action and tend to seek help only when pressured by others. This is the stage that most readers are likely to be stuck in. The third stage is the *preparation* stage, during which a person begins to talk openly about their LBA relationship, seek advice about what they can do to protect themselves, and develop a plan of action. Without doubt, this is the most courageous step—acknowledging to themselves and others that they have a problem that needs fixing. Fourth, the individual takes specific, concrete steps—*action*—to set about not just surviving the LBA relationship but rather to recover from the damage already sustained. For example, the person may have entered a counseling relationship or taken legal steps to restrain a loved one from further physical abuse. Finally, there is the *maintenance* stage, in which you have achieved your goal of becoming a non-victim in an LBA relationship and now are doing everything possible to hold on to the gains you have made.

It is not clear what moves people from one stage of readiness to another. Your age, personality factors, how much support you have for making a change, whether your loved one is capable of physical violence, and whether his/her anger outbursts are episodic or chronic, are all likely to influence your intention to move forward in resolving your LBA relationship. What is clear, though, is that people often do not progress linearly from one stage to the next, but rather cycle back sometimes through previous stages. You may begin to make small positive changes in how you cope with your angry loved one, but then have second thoughts and take a step back, reconsidering your options. The good news is that each time you move forward, then back, you learn from your mistakes, so that you can try something different next time. The key to long-term success is persistence!

**Take a minute and assess where your starting point is. Using the definitions above, place an X on the line below to signify how ready you are for change:**

_____

| No Intention | Preintention | Preparation | Action | Maintenance |

The vast majority of readers will find themselves in either the preintention or preparation stage. If reading this book does nothing else but move you to the next stage toward action, then the investment will have been worth it.

## I Think I Can, I Think I Can

When I was a small child, I loved to read and one of my favorite stories was *The Little Engine That Could*. Those of you who have read this book will recall that the Little Blue Engine was able to carry the stranded toys and dolls over the mountain only by repeating to herself, "I think I can. I think I can." This little engine saved the day, in sharp contrast to another engine that earlier refused to help, instead rumbling off down the tracks saying, "I can not. I can not." The moral of this wonderful, timeless story is unmistakable: If you believe you are capable of succeeding as some insurmountable task, you will.

A quarter of a century ago, Stanford University psychologist Albert Bandura introduced the principle of *perceived self-efficacy* as a key element in the process by which human beings change behavior.[2] Perceived self-efficacy doesn't have so much to do with whether particular actions—for example, the seven steps that follow—will lead to the eventual resolution of a problem, but rather to a belief that you can successfully implement those steps. A person low on self-efficacy is likely to concede that reaching out for support (Chapter Seven) or beginning to set limits on how much anger they are willing to tolerate (Chapter Nine) would benefit them, but he/she does not see him/herself as capable of doing either.

One reason people often do not have confidence in their ability to succeed at a self-help program centered around the issue of relationship anger is that they have been so focused on the task of fixing their loved one's anger that they have devoted little time and energy to attempting to change their own behavior. Because of this, they have no direct experience in successfully caring for themselves which they in turn can use as a basis for believing themselves capable of change. As Bandura also points out, emotional arousal can affect self-efficacy in that situations that produce high arousal (fear) in people tend to leave them doubting their ability to cope effectively with that particular situation. Toxic anger, I think we would all agree, is one type of experience that is likely to create a state of high arousal in those to whom it is directed. It's hard to feel confident when you are scared for your life!

**To assess your own sense of self-efficacy, respond to the following statement by placing an X over the response that best describes how you feel right this moment:**

**I believe I can learn to do what it takes to protect myself from my _____'s toxic anger.**

| Not Really | Not Sure | Maybe | Probably | Absolutely |

Readers can reasonably expect to build a sense of self-efficacy as they move from one step to another in our seven-step program of recovery. As one of our clients put it, this program not only "opened my eyes as to what I was allowing other people to do to me, it helped me gain respect for myself."

## What's the Upside of Change?

Human beings, like all living creatures, need incentives to change. There are incentives (benefits) and disincentives (costs) associated with all behaviors. In my earlier book, *Anger-Free—Ten Basic Steps to Managing Your Anger,* I focused exclusively on the disincentives associated with toxic anger. Here, I want instead to have you consider the possible benefits (upside) of changing your status in the LBA relationship from that of victim to non-victim.

To illustrate, let us return to the stories in Chapter One. By separating himself from his brother's anger, Jerry was able to preserve the "five or six good memories I have of him," which he was afraid he would lose forever if they ever got together again. Once Sherri quit trying to fix her son's rageful behavior and began focusing on her own well-being, she felt much less emotionally "drained" all the time and she quit reacting so angrily herself. Donald felt that his family was "safer" from his father's abusive anger once he finally took a stand. Marilyn feels relieved every time she walks through her front door and doesn't have to see her ex-husband's "angry face staring back at me." Tony has not been to a medical care facility lately as a result of physical abuse suffered at the hands of his rageful partner. And Victor—what benefits have come his way now that he is no longer a victim of his wife's incessant anger? Well, according to Victor, he now:

- is generally less frantic and desperate than before

- feels less intimidated than he did before

- sleeps better than he did before

- has reconnected with his old "competent" self at work

- has widened his circle of supportive friends

- is in the best mood he has been in for many years

- has discontinued all psychiatric medication

- has greatly improved relationships with all of his children

Does any of this sound the least bit appealing to you? What other benefits would you expect from your efforts to change your role in the LBA relationship?

1. _____

2. _____

3. _____

4. _____

5. _____

Relationship change can be both painful and risky. There has to be something in it for you.

## Hardy Is as Hardy Does

We have a water pond in our backyard that freezes solid each winter. Somehow, the goldfish survive under a block of ice that measures twenty-two inches across and eighteen inches deep. Every spring, when I once again see them swimming freely about, I am amazed. How hardy those little creatures are!

Personality "hardiness" in humans, according to psychologists Salvatore Maddi and Suzanne Kobasa, goes a long way toward minimizing the adverse effects of everyday life stress. Hardy people, in effect, survive hard times. Highly stressed executives, for example, who are also hardy exhibit one-third to one-half as much stress-related illness—hypertension, peptic ulcer, psoriasis—as do stressed executives who are low on hardiness.[3] Maddi and Kobasa define hardiness as a combination of three things: (a) a sense of personal control over stressful life circumstances; (b) a deep sense of commitment and purpose in daily activities; and, (c) a tendency to view stress as a challenge and opportunity for personal growth, rather than a crisis.

All three components appear critical to whether individuals succeed at self-directed change. Hardy personalities accept the challenge of a problematic relationship—in this case, one filled with too much anger—rather than avoiding it. They believe that their future is within their (internal) control and they leave nothing to chance or fate. And they are actively committed to—as opposed to alienated from—their own cause. Non-hardy individuals, on the other hand, are more likely to feel powerless in response to their loved one's anger and to engage in attempts to deny, avoid, or escape such stress.

**How would you rate yourself on a scale from 1 (Extremely Non-Hardy) to 10 (Extremely Hardy)? (Circle one)**

| 1 | 2 | 3 | 4 | 5 | 6 | 7 | 8 | 9 | 10 |
|---|---|---|---|---|---|---|---|---|---|
| Low | | | | | | | | | High |

## Learned Helplessness: The Worst of the Worst

Some years ago, a prominent New York attorney killed his young daughter in a fit of rage and then went off to work as if nothing had happened. All the while, his wife looked on and did nothing to protect the child or to get her medical assistance following the brutal beating. The main question on the minds of most Americans at the time, interestingly, was not "How could this man do such a thing?" but rather, "How could a mother just stand by and let it happen without lifting a finger?" The explanation, it turns out, was simple: this mother, like millions of other abused women, suffered from an extreme form of *learned helplessness*. Learned helplessness is doubly important because it can be a form of damage resulting from an LBA relationship, as well as a major barrier to self-help.

According to Dr. Martin Seligman, former president of the American Psychological Association and noted researcher, learned helplessness occurs when a person has been conditioned through years of failed attempts at coping to think and act as if nothing they do will make a difference in the outcome of any distressful or potentially damaging life situation. They feel powerless to change either themselves or the situation. A person suffering from learned helplessness, for example, will not actively seek reemployment when they are out of work; nor will they, as in the case illustrated above, act in their own behalf (or that of someone else) when they find themselves on the receiving end of a loved one's toxic, lethal anger. They have become victims, emotionally paralyzed and totally passive bystanders in the path of true danger.

Human beings do not start out life in a state of learned helplessness. Life teaches them to be this way. Children who suffer physical and sexual abuse, those raised in alcoholic homes, those who have life-threatening illnesses, those living in impoverished environments, all quickly develop a feeling of helplessness in dealing with the world around them. Once learned, this mind-set is very difficult, some would say impossible, to overcome and it can lead to the worst-case scenario in an LBA relationship—death. Many of the "real people" I have presented as examples thus far in this book had almost gotten to this point of helplessness when I first met them. But all had managed in some way or another to escape feeling totally helpless and hopeless, either by fighting back or by terminating the LBA relationship altogether. Sherri was close to the end of her (emotional) rope after years of putting up with her son's abusive anger. Donald, even though he was now in his forties and a successful man in all other respects, was continuing to feel like a helpless child every time his father flew into yet another rage. Sarah found herself conflicted by a fear that her angry boyfriend would abandon her, while at the same time wishing he would. And Victor, a "man's man," was only one small step away from a complete nervous breakdown as a result of his futile efforts to deal with ten years of marital anger. The good news is that each of these people was able to act to remove him/herself from harm's way before it was too late—before he/she experienced the worst of the worst.

How close are you to the feeling of learned helplessness?

———

Now that you have assessed your potential for change, all you need is a self-help program aimed at increasing your sense of personal safety, helping you recover from damage already done to you by your LBA relationship(s), and, above all else, restoring you to the status of a non-victim. The remainder of this book is devoted to just such a program.

# CHAPTER SEVEN

# STEP ONE: REACHING OUT

Human beings are, with rare exception, incapable of surviving major stress or making meaningful change in their lives without the help of others. Psychologists have long touted the importance of supportive relationships in mediating the negative effect of stress on mental and physical health. The more support one has during difficult times, the less one seems to be adversely affected. Dr. Redford Williams at Duke University Medical Center noted, for example, that patients undergoing coronary angiography were three times more likely to die from heart disease within five years if they were unmarried or could not identify a "confidant" with whom they could share their troubles.[1] Interestingly, this striking difference in survival rates remained even when the investigators took into account the severity of disease suffered by each individual. A similar study of women experiencing "high stress" pregnancies found that they were three times more likely to have babies born with complications if they had little or no support from families and friends in the months leading up to delivery as compared to other women with stressful pregnancies who enjoyed a large measure of support throughout.[2]

Because of the all-important buffering effect that social support provides to individuals undergoing intense stress, I believe the crucial first step necessary to protect a person in an LBA relationship from further harm and to help that person embark on a healing process is to have them reach out to others for a helping hand. As University of Michigan sociologist James House suggests, that helping hand typically involves "a flow of one or more of four things between people": emotional concern, instrumental aid, informational support or advice, and appraisal.[3]

Expressing *emotional concern* involves such things as active listening, physical touch, providing a much needed opportunity to vent one's pent-up feelings, or simply caring enough to ask the victim of an LBA relationship, "Are you okay?"

*Instrumental aid* means doing something tangible to help that person, e.g., taking him/her to the emergency room after he/she has been physically assaulted or buying him/her a book on how to deal with abusive relationships.

*Informational support* offers the person guidance as to what they should do next to ensure their personal safety and emotional well-being. I remember once receiving a late-night call from the wife of a distant relative who asked me what she should do, having just been assaulted by her husband. My advice was simple: get yourself and the children out of the house immediately; then call the police and press charges. The woman seemed stunned, replying

"But he's your _____." "I know," I said, "and I love him, but that's still the best advice I can give you." Being supportive is not always telling the other person what they want to hear.

And, finally, *appraisal* involves giving the person in need honest, objective, and corrective feedback about the things they are doing to facilitate both the continuation and/or escalation of the LBA relationship. Again, providing an outside perspective on a troublesome relationship, while supportive, may not always be well received initially, but it is what the person needs to hear.

Unfortunately, having a loving relationship with an angry person erodes one's support system. For one thing, the victim of an LBA relationship must look elsewhere for much-needed support, as they cannot realistically expect to receive comfort and advice from their very angry partner. Perpetrators of toxic anger tend to lack sensitivity, compassion, and concern for others—remember, rage is "blind."

## The Need to Feel Human

Amanda, a forty-eight-year-old housewife, was the object of her husband's alcoholic rage for almost twenty years. "He was verbally explosive when he was drinking, and he was never sober—not one day—for seventeen years," she admitted. He would demean her constantly, calling her "stupid, idiot, and weak minded," and as his drinking intensified over the years he eventually attacked her physically. At the same time, her teenage daughter also became abusively angry. "It all started when she was about fourteen years old. She would fly into fits of anger and hit and kick me, leaving me bruised on my legs, arms, and chest. It was horrible!" Amanda was obviously fighting a two-front war, constantly attacked by the two people she loved the most.

So where could she go for support? She tried talking to her daughter about her husband's anger, but her daughter was unsympathetic: "You stayed here; it's your fault if you get hurt!" She tried talking to her husband about her daughter's anger, but he gave the same response: "It's all your fault!" So she turned to her next-door neighbor. "She was the only one I could talk to at the time. I could go over there any time, sometimes several times a day, and cry, talk, yell. She was on my side. She understood how I was feeling, and she could see that all this was leading me down a very dangerous trail."

"Did your neighbor give you any advice?" I asked. Jokingly, she replied: "Yeah, 'LEAVE, LEAVE, LEAVE.'" She also suggested tying Amanda's husband up and beating the daylights out of him. "She was just what I needed. She was the one saying the things I felt like doing. She was a real comfort."

Amanda did not leave the marriage, but things are somewhat better now. Her husband has been sober for three years and he is more irritable these days than angry. Her daughter has occasional flares of temper, but is no longer physically assaultive. Which is good, because her neighbor moved away and she has no one else to reach out to for support. "I only had two other friends, and they both died last year. Now I just talk to my animals."

Amanda remembers those years, when she was all alone in an angry family. She felt as if, she says, "I had nowhere to go to feel like a human being" except next door. Often she thinks that things would have turned out better in the long run if she'd taken her friend's advice, but at the very least she's thankful that her friend was there when she most needed her. "I'd have killed myself if not for her. I was that desperate, that unsure of myself, that weak minded, as my husband like to call me."

Remember Sherri from Chapter One? When asked about what sort of support she had to deal with her angry son, she indicated that she was blessed by having a girlfriend of twenty years, who was a veritable "lifeline" in her efforts to maintain her sanity. Interestingly, the two women have lived in different parts of the country for most of that time—over fifteen years. Sherri struggled in her LBA relationship with her son, while her friend struggled in an LBA relationship with an alcoholic husband. They encouraged each other to make healthier, sometimes difficult, choices about how to protect themselves from rageful loved ones. Sherri was also fortunate to have a supportive husband, who was always there for her at times of crisis, but it was this long-distance relationship that sustained her the most. She summed up the importance of their relationship by saying, "Sometimes just having someone say, 'We're going to get through this—we're going to be okay' is all that you need." And that's what they were able to do for each other.

Because social support is so important to a person in an LBA relationship, probably those that suffer the most are young children, because more often than not they lack the social network that can offer the emotional assistance they need. Jerry, the forty-three-year-old police officer I introduced in Chapter One, is a good example of what happens when children are the victims of LBA relationships. Jerry was literally terrorized on a daily basis by his brother Sam's rage, but he had no one to reach out to for a helping hand. His father had abandoned the family years before and his mother (who also had problems with her temper) was struggling in the role of single parent. The family had little or no social connection to neighbors, friends, or extended family—they were a family alone.

Jerry learned all too quickly to survive without depending on anyone but himself. He became adept at being a loner, an alienated personality who to this day has difficulty confiding in those closest to him. I asked his wife of twenty years if he had ever shared with her anything about those awful years of suffering at the hands of his brother's anger. "Not really," she said. "If someone brings up the issue of anger, he'll talk about Sam, but it's like he's telling a story about something that happened to someone else. He'll even joke about his brother's rage. I think that's his way of saying it didn't really affect him, but I know it did."

Ironically, Jerry is eager to lend a helping hand to others. He is sensitive to the needs of others—his wife, children, neighbors, friends, employees—and will reach out to be supportive in any way he can without any expectation of reciprocity. This is his biggest problem: he knows how to give, but not to receive. And all that started because of an LBA relationship early in life. Building a foundation of emotional support is crucial to surviving loving but angry relationships and to be able to take the steps necessary to stop being a lifelong victim of toxic anger.

# Seven Things to Know about Support

**1.** *Social support should be a facet of everyday life.* I lived on the Texas coast for several years and I was taught early on that "the time to prepare for a hurricane is before it hits!" And so it is with support. Building a network of supportive relationships to be used in times of personal crisis is one key to a healthy life. When you reach out for help, you want someone there to answer, right? Every little positive exchange (taking a good friend out to lunch for no special reason; sending someone a 'thinking of you' card) we have with our support team in the course of everyday life is an investment in our future as well as theirs. I keep a card on my desk at work with the phone numbers of lifelong members of my support team, people I call in times of crisis and who in turn call me. Sometimes, when I have an unexpected break in my day, I ring up one of these special people and say "Hi, how are you?" Their response: "Funny, I was just thinking about calling you."

Most of the individuals I see who end up in counseling for LBA relationships do so, in large part, because they have no one to reach out to other than me.

The size of one's support network is obviously important. The smaller our network, the less opportunity we have to solicit or receive support. In that sense, it's a game of numbers—with the most critical number being "zero." The truly isolated partner in an LBA relationship is the most vulnerable and the one most likely to be severely damaged by toxic anger. In working with mothers who have abused their children, I almost always found them to be women who had few adult (supportive) relationships other than their angry, abusive spouse—that's what made them so dangerous.

2. *Support helps fulfill the need to belong.* We humans are social animals and we have an inborn need to belong, to be part of something greater than ourselves. Meaningful social ties are just as vital to sustaining physical (biological) life as food, water, or the air we breathe. This is, in fact, one of the biggest problems with LBA relationships; they disturb some of the most important social connections in our lives—those with our loved ones. Rage serves to dehumanize such relationships. As the angry person sees it, "That person is not worthy of my respect. They do not deserve a kind word or a gesture of forgiveness. It doesn't matter if I hurt them—they're not human." Support offers an all-important counter-message to this contemptuous orientation; it rehumanizes people who find themselves isolated and shut off from meaningful social exchange.

3. *Support must be reciprocal.* Support should be a "give and take" process. We cannot simply reach out to others during difficult times; we must also be there when they need us. While members of your support team may not have anger issues that they are grappling with, they most assuredly have (or will have) other issues—a child on drugs, a parent with Alzheimer's, being out of work, death of a pet—that they require help with from time to time. Be there for them as well. The surest way to burn out supportive relationships is to fail to reciprocate.

But remember, a relationship must go both ways, which means you can't just be a "giver," either. Remember Jerry who was a very giving person but was reluctant to ask for help himself? And, Victor, who thought for ten years that he was strong enough to withstand his wife's incessant rage all by himself while at the same time being a supportive father and friend to others? One ended up with a near-fatal heart attack and the other on the verge of a nervous breakdown, both before age fifty! In general, men have more difficulty with this end of the "give and take" process than do women.

4. *Support can be both general and specific.* A generally supportive person will be there for you no matter what your need. Others can be supportive for certain things but not others. This is an important distinction because not everyone will feel comfortable in lending a helping hand where anger is involved, especially if it rises to the intensity of rage or expresses itself in personal violence. It has been my experience that even mental-health counselors tend to be more willing to take on clients who are anxious or depressed than those that present with anger problems. Specific support is without doubt the most helpful to the person in an LBA relationship, just as support from a co-worker is more helpful when one is dealing with work-related stresses. For one thing, the supportive person who has, in today's parlance, "been there, done that" can empathize (feel *with* you), whereas the individual providing general support can only be sympathetic (feel *for* you) to your plight. Second, specific support can also be more helpful because the person offering it has prior experience in dealing with LBA relationships and you can, thus, learn

from their successes as well as their mistakes. Ideally, your support team should involve both of these types of support.

5. *Support that is unrecognized or unused is unhelpful.* Not everyone recognizes the support that is available to them for help with LBA relationships. Men, for example, often do not consider potential sources of support outside their marriage or biological family. While they will rely on other males as sources of recreation or to help with non-relationship tasks—building a garage or moving a heavy object— they are far less likely than women to reach out for help when dealing with an angry loved one. Many men would, in fact, see such behavior as a way of "losing face" within the competitive male world. Maybe this is one reason why men live seven fewer years than women on average? Another reason many of us fail to recognize support is that we depend on it so little that we simply forget it is there. Or, as we have already noted, we failed to do our part in previous mutually supportive relationships so that that source of support slowly but surely disappears. For support to be continually present in our lives, it must be used and nurtured. It cannot be ignored and neglected.

6. *The ability to give and receive support depends on past experiences and personality.* Introverts, for instance, are less likely to give and receive support than are extroverts. Introverts draw much of their support—along with energy and creativity—from within themselves (I'm my own best friend; I seek my own counsel), rather than from the external world of other people. Extroverts, on the other hand, get all their needs met, as well as their inspiration, from

their dealings with fellow human beings. People who are trusting and open with the world at large are more likely to reach out in times of need, as compared to those who are closed and suspicious of others. Pessimists are less likely to reach out than optimists. Why? Because they assume no one will respond to their need. Victims of early life abuse—emotional, physical, or sexual—are less likely to recognize and utilize support because of fear they will once again be rejected or hurt. Depressed people are less likely to solicit support than nondepressed folks. Type A personalities (aggressive, impatient, cynical) are less likely to reach out than their Type B counterparts. And, as ironic as it may seem, people who have had an easy, uneventful life prior to finding themselves in an LBA relationship may not actually know how to reach out for support, as it represents a type of "new" behavior on their part, something not necessary before. This was Sarah's (Chapter One) problem. She had never been exposed to "toxic" anger before and she didn't know how to respond at first other than to hope that things would get better.

7. *So long as you are breathing, it's never too late to ask for help.* Anne (Chapter Five) spent the first sixty years of her life trying in every way she could think of to remain "invisible," afraid that others would discover what her angry father had always known— that she was a stupid and unworthy person. Only recently has she found a kindred spirit, a friend her own age, who also had an LBA relationship with a "difficult" father. "We find ourselves wondering why we never liked ourselves and now we know," she said. The operative term here is *we*.

## Step One: Assemble Your Support Team

Make a list of people you think (or know from past experience) will support you in your efforts to free yourself from the harmful effects of an LBA relationship. Beside each name, list the type(s) of support you have received or are likely to receive from that person (EC = emotional concern, IA = instrumental aid, A = advice, AF = appraisal/feedback), and give an example of how that type of support has been or might be expressed by that team member. Next, indicate whether their support is general (G) or specific (S) to the problem of dealing with a loved one's anger. Then ask yourself, "How long has it been since I talked to that person?"

Keep in mind that a support team can consist of only one other person. What matters most is the quality, consistency, and availability of supportive relationships, not the actual number. If, after much thought, you cannot identify even one person that you can reach out to at this time, then you may want to consider enlisting some professional support. Also, check to see what is available in the way of community support, e.g., services to abused and battered women. Contact your local mental-health agency or health department to inquire about such groups, as well as the offices of local physicians, mental-health providers (clinical psychologists, psychiatrists, social workers), and clergy. Anger is a less identified problem in most communities and has received far less formal attention than other major problems—drug and alcohol abuse, single parenting, depression, gambling, eating disorders, heart disease, multiple sclerosis—but maybe there is something out there to meet your needs. Or maybe you yourself would be interested in starting such a group.

## SOCIAL SUPPORT

| SOURCE | TYPE | HOW EXPRESSED | G/S | HOW LONG |
|--------|------|---------------|-----|----------|
| Tom | E | Let me ventilate | S | Month |
| | AF | Told me I'm a good person and deserve better. | | |
| | | | | |
| | | | | |
| | | | | |
| | | | | |
| | | | | |
| | | | | |
| | | | | |
| | | | | |
| | | | | |

Now let's move on to Step Two and see if we can help you get your mind right.

# CHAPTER EIGHT

# STEP TWO:
# GET YOUR MIND RIGHT

Paul Newman, in the movie *Cool Hand Luke*, plays the role of a rebellious prison inmate who is determined to escape his captors no matter what the consequences. The guards, frustrated by his refusal to cooperate, finally resort to severe physical punishment. As Newman lies exhausted and beaten in a makeshift grave, he begs not to be hurt anymore. A guard responds, "You got your mind right, Luke?" "Yeah, I got it right. I got it right, boss," he cries out, "I got my mind right." But he doesn't. So he tries to escape one last time and he is caught and killed. The lesson here being: *If you don't get your mind right, you can get hurt even more than you already are.*

## SELF-ASSESSMENT

Before we apply this lesson to LBA relationships, I first want you to complete this brief questionnaire regarding common beliefs people have about the interplay between love and anger in human relationships. Put a number corresponding to one of the answers below in front of each of the statements listed. Be honest with yourself.

To what extent do you believe the following?
0 = I do not believe this is true.
1 = I somewhat believe this statement to be true.
2 = I moderately believe this statement to be true.
3 = I strongly believe that this is true.

_____ 1. Love will prevail even in a relationship with an angry person.

_____ 2. If the angry person loves me enough, they will change.

_____ 3. Anger is fleeting, but love is forever.

_____ 4. As long as two people love each other, nothing else matters.

_____ 5. Loving someone means not making them angry.

_____ 6. If he/she is angry with me, it means he/she actually cares about me.

_____ 7. A loving relationship will make a person less angry.

———— 8. **If someone I love becomes angry with me, it means I have done something wrong.**

**Now add up your scores:** ——————— . **The maximum score you can obtain is 24. The higher your score, the more you need to get your mind right.**

## Common Myths about Love and Anger

Many people are virtual prisoners of LBA relationships because of the beliefs they hold about these two strong, opposing emotions. My experience over the years has convinced me that it is these "mental traps" that too often keep people from taking proactive, corrective steps to avoid the damaging effects of their loved one's toxic anger. Only by becoming aware of how attached you are to these beliefs and by challenging the credibility of each can you move on through the seven-step recovery program.

By far, the most commonly held myth is that: *A loving relationship will make a person less angry.* Forty-seven percent of those people we surveyed rated this as a moderately or strongly held belief, including, amazingly, 43 percent of those who had previously been in or were currently in an LBA relationship. The truth is that nothing you do can make another person less angry, try as you may. It is fine to love them, but don't fool yourself into believing that your love is powerful enough to curb their temper. Early in their LBA relationships, all the people whose stories I featured in Chapter One felt this way. You cannot possibly love a son any more than Sherri has over the years, and yet her son is still having "anger fits" seventeen years after he started. You cannot love a father more than Donald has his whole life and yet his father is still raging at age seventy-five. Sarah loved her boyfriend so much she was willing to marry him despite his abusive anger. These people all learned the hard way just how unrealistic and fanciful this belief is.

The second most widely held myth about love and anger is: *Anger is fleeting, but love is forever.* Thirty-four percent of our respondents firmly believe this. But they are wrong. As I noted in Chapter Two, for almost a fourth of the population (23.1 percent), anger is anything but fleeting. On the contrary, it is a chronic problem that manifests itself daily throughout their lives. Victor's wife's anger was certainly not fleeting; it lasted for over a decade, long past his ability to keep loving her. Donald's father's rage has lasted to the point where Donald admits there is no question that it has permanently "tainted" their relationship. Sarah thought she would be happily married to Todd, but she's not. The only love that Jerry holds for his brother is that embedded in a few ancient childhood memories. These people all found out the hard way that toxic, pathologic anger can far outlast love, no matter how strong and heartfelt.

The next most strongly held myth about love/anger is: *Love will prevail even in a relationship with an angry person.* Thirty-one percent share this belief. This is actually a correlate of the previous belief—if something prevails it lasts forever. If this is true, then why is Victor's love for his wife "dead"? Why aren't Sarah and Todd going to spend their life together like they initially intended? Why has

Jerry not tried to contact his brother all these years? And why did Tony choose to move far away from his beloved partner? The answer to all these questions is the same: *If anger prevails, love does not!*

Twenty-eight percent of those surveyed agreed with the statement: *If the angry person loves me enough, they will change.* Ironically, many on the receiving end of an LBA relationship steadfastly remain in harm's way as a test of the other person's love. *Surely,* they think, *my _____ will eventually realize just how much they love me and they will stop being so angry.* What they want is some genuine empathy, some sensitivity, some caring, some compassion, some concern for their needs and welfare—all ingredients of love. But these attributes and behaviors tend to be lacking in highly angry people. They cannot give you what they don't have. Also, the idea that their loved one doesn't love them enough to stop his/her outrageous behavior is unthinkable. Better to be abused than unloved, right? Wrong.

One out of six of our respondents believe that: *As long as two people love each other, nothing else matters.* Try telling that to Sherri, who lived a very socially restricted life for years because she couldn't go anywhere where she thought her angry son would not be accepted or it would be too difficult a situation for him to handle. Try convincing Donald, who has to work hard these days to continue feeling love for his father, of that. Try getting Anne to rethink her decision not to visit her father in the nursing home before his death by suggesting that the lifetime of rage she endured should not have really mattered. Of course other things besides love matter; personal safety matters, health matters, sanity matters, happiness matters, self-respect matters, dignity matters, peace of mind matters. And none of these things are possible in the context of LBA relationships.

Why is the belief that *loving someone means not making them angry* a myth? Simple: Whether we love someone or not, we cannot make them angry. Certainly, we can provide them with any number of opportunities to experience anger, but whether they respond with anger depends on them—their personality, how much they have had to drink, their mood, their stress level—not us. Interestingly, this is the belief that most angry people champion themselves; it is their way of holding you responsible for their anger. And what is wrong with the idea that *if someone I love gets angry with me, it means I've done something wrong?* Wrong is a perception, not a fact. What is wrong for you might be right for someone else. Deciding that someone has acted wrongly is just another way of saying, "You haven't done what I want. You haven't met my needs the way I think you should. You haven't let me win or control the situation that we find ourselves in." Anger may signal that you have done something to displease your loved one, but that does not make what you have said or done wrong. Lastly, why is it a mistake to believe that *if my loved one is angry with me, it means they actually care about me?* As we noted in Chapter Three, the toxic anger one sees in LBA relationships is part of the anger-contempt-disgust emotional triad. Your loved one, in effect, is not only angry with you, he/she is repulsed by you, finds you worthless, and disrespects you. Isn't this the opposite of "caring" for or about you? Bottom line: Angry loved ones care more about themselves than they do about you!

## Myths Die Hard

The beliefs human beings have about life form early on as a result of socialization experiences and cultural pressures and they are not easily changed. We live in a culture that, on the one hand, romanticizes love ("Love conquers all!") but, on the other hand, has little to say or at the very least is ambivalent about anger among its citizenry. This explains our finding that those persons who claim no direct experience with abusive anger have the highest scores on our questionnaire about the interplay between love and anger, while those who are currently in LBA relationships have the lowest scores. Those who are being damaged by these abusive relationships learn all too quickly the difference between the "ideal" versus "reality." And what about those surveyed who had prior experience with an LBA relationship but are currently free of such abuse? Interestingly, their scores are closer to those who have never yet encountered an LBA relationship. To me, this suggests that these myths die hard, and that once a person is out of an LBA relationship, they regrettably revert back to their old way of thinking. This may well explain why so many people cycle from one LBA relationship to another.

———

Mike, a twenty-four-year-old college graduate, fell in love for the first time three years ago. He has many fond memories of that time together, as he and his girlfriend, Lisa, had many similar interests and they "played well" together in terms of recreational pursuits. By Mike's account, things were good about 80 percent of the time.

But there was an increasing dark side to their relationship. With great regularity—every five or six months—Lisa would suddenly, for no apparent reason, go into an unprovoked rage, lash out violently at Mike, and then abruptly terminate their relationship. Each time, Mike was caught off guard and was thus unable to defend himself from the onslaught of her anger. And each time he was emotionally devastated. Typically, things would quiet down for several days and then he and Lisa would reconnect and the next cycle would begin. After each "explosion," he would say that he couldn't take being hurt this way again, but he would inevitably resume the relationship because he honestly believed that maybe this time things would somehow be better.

When he looks back on the relationship, Mike said he would have scored 19 out of a possible 24 on the beliefs questionnaire when he first got together with Lisa, but now after all he had been through, he scores a 7. Being in an LBA relationship certainly taught Mike a lot about love and anger. Even now, however, he holds firm to three of these misguided beliefs: (1) If the angry person loves me enough, she will change; (2) If she is angry with me, it means she actually cares about me; and (3) A loving relationship will make a person less angry. Myths, it would seem, die hard.

## Step Two: Cognitive Restructuring

Psychologists refer to thoughts, beliefs, and expectations collectively as cognitions and their principle strategy for overcoming bogus, irrational cognitions is *cognitive restructuring*. The goal here is to help you change (restructure) the way you think about love and anger, thereby reducing or eliminating altogether those "mental traps" that keep you stuck in a damaging and potentially lethal relationship with a loved one.

So how do you do that? The first technique you can employ is thought-stopping. You simply say STOP! whenever you find yourself thinking one of those irrational thoughts you have identified on the questionnaire. You can say it aloud (which is generally more effective) or silently to yourself, whichever you are more comfortable with given the situation you are in at the time. The goal is to initially interrupt this type of maladaptive thinking and in turn to substitute more realistic beliefs. The second technique is called rational emotive therapy (RET),[1] which involves challenging the false belief and replacing it with a more realistic thought. The following is an example:

False Belief: Anger is fleeting, but love is forever.

Challenge: Not really. Some people bear grudges forever. If love lasts forever, there wouldn't be so many divorces and abused children, would there?

Replacement Thought: Too much anger can certainly keep love from lasting forever.

Now, you try it. Explore some of your own myths about your love and your loved one's anger, challenge them, and then replace them with more realistic, healthy thoughts. Where did each of these beliefs originate? What evidence do you have to support them? What evidence do you have that argues against them? Are you the only one who thinks like this?

Remember, the way you think is a personal choice and you can choose to restructure your thinking (get your mind right) any time you like. And don't forget to use your support team. That's what kept Sherri and her girlfriend sane for the past twenty years, using each other to rethink their LBA relationships with a raging child and an alcoholic, belligerent husband. Try to be open-minded when others tell you what they think, rather than engaging in a concerted effort to defend or justify your way of thinking. If your beliefs hold up to the challenge, by all means keep them. If they don't hold up, maybe it is time to make a change. When all is said and done, beliefs may be the most dangerous weapons of all—ones that, if we are not careful, we end up using against ourselves.

MYTH #1:_____

Challenge: _____

Replacement: _____


MYTH #2:_____

Challenge: _____

Replacement: _____

MYTH #3:_____

Challenge: _____

Replacement: _____

MYTH #4:_____

Challenge: _____

Replacement: _____

MYTH #5:_____

Challenge: _____

Replacement: _____

Now let's move on to the next step and consider the importance of setting limits. But on whom should we set those limits?

# CHAPTER NINE

# STEP THREE: SET LIMITS

Her name was Naomi and she was an attractive, intelligent, extremely articulate woman in her late forties, hardly the type of person one might expect to be on the receiving end of toxic anger. At the time she told me her story, she had been divorced for almost eight years and yet, as she talked about her angry, at times violent, ex-husband, you could still see the fear in her eyes and hear the pain in her voice about a time in her life that she longed to forget.

Naomi had married a man she truly loved—an active, happy, dynamic man—when she was barely twenty. She remembers having a glimpse of what was in store for her later on when her then fiancé got drunk at a party and viciously attacked one of his longtime friends, a woman. But he was very remorseful afterward, attributing his rage to too much alcohol, and Naomi was quick to accept his apology. In an attempt to "fix" his anger problem, however, she did insist that he refrain from excessive drinking as they proceeded toward marriage, hoping that this was just an isolated event.

But she was wrong. What followed was fourteen years of unbridled rage: "I recall once having a discussion with him and I must have said something that didn't suit him, because without warning he grabbed me by my shirt and pulled me toward him with such force that it ripped the shirt completely off me. He brought me right to his face where he was so angry that he spit on me—he was literally foaming at the mouth!"

This and countless other episodes of rage were always followed by remorse, as well as other explanations of why her husband could not control his temper. He had, he argued, come from a family in which rage was the order of the day, and so, like his father before him, he could not help himself when he got mad. And, as always, Naomi was tolerant and forgiving.

Her focus throughout her marriage remained on her husband rather than herself. She tried appeasing him to no avail. "He had this checklist of things that he would go down until he found something I hadn't done and then he would get very angry. It was as if he was looking to pick a fight, for an excuse to lose his temper. And there was always something." She tried finding neutral ground on which they could relate without anger, but she ultimately came to realize that "there was no neutral ground with a person like this."

She tried "shutting up" and not saying anything about his outrageous behavior, but that did not do any good. She tried being "worthy" of his love by striving to meet all of his unreasonable expectations and demands, but always seemed to fall short. She tried helping him "save face" and avoid the shame that should have followed his violent behavior. She tried being "too kind" to this man who terrorized her with relentless, utter contempt. She tried doing "special" things for him, for example the time when she spent the entire day sprucing up the yard to please him while he was off on a fishing trip with friends. Characteristically, when he returned home, he took one look at the beautiful yard and remarked angrily, "I hope you don't think this entitles you to any special treatment. Besides, you look like hell!"

What Naomi, of course, failed to do was set limits on her own self: on her willingness to endure year after year of toxic anger; on her tolerance for undeserved abusive behavior; on her own insistence that this was a problem that she could remedy without anyone else's help; on her health (she suffered from migraine headaches made worse by the threat of constant abuse); and perhaps most of all, on her continuing love for a man who only brought pain and fear into her life.

It was only during the tenth year of her marriage, when a close friend finally found the courage to say to her, "You know you don't have to live like this," that she began to protect herself from further harm. How did she do this? "I began to dissociate myself from the social group—including his family and inner circle of friends—that had long enabled his violent behavior. I began to spend more time alone, to establish a lifestyle separate from his, and to encourage him to do more things without me, which he was all too ready to do. The more he was gone, the less anger I had to endure." Her efforts to set limits on how exposed she was to her husband's anger had immediate benefit to her children as well. "We were all able to function much better without the anger when he wasn't around."

This step turned out to be the beginning of what was a difficult decision on Naomi's part to eventually divorce her husband. Even with all his anger, she still loved her husband "for all the reasons I married him in the first place," but she now understood that she could no longer live with him and be well.

## You Can Set Limits and You Need to Do It Now

To paraphrase an old saying, if I had a dollar for every time I heard someone say, "I can't stand his/her anger anymore," I would be comfortably retired by now.

I have found, after thirty-five years of observing and trying to change human behavior, that, in fact, people can stand just about any type of aversive (painful) experience known to man, despite protesting otherwise. And they can stand such pain for long periods of time, even unto death. Some of these painful experiences are not changeable (e.g., chronic intractable back pain); others are. The suffering that accompanies toxic anger in an LBA relationship is changeable. But, before this can happen, a person like Naomi must realize that the crucial question is not, "How long can I stand my husband's anger?"—after all she put up with it for fourteen years— but rather, "How long do I *want* to continue being a victim of marital rage?" The word *can* conveys an ability to continue experiencing something, whereas the word *want* speaks to the issue of motivation or will. For the first decade of her marriage, Naomi wanted to remain married, but "fix" her husband's anger, and only after a good friend reminded her that she didn't have to live this way did she realize she could change (improve) her situation.

(Check one) At this point, I _____ will or _____ will not continue to be the victim of my _____'s toxic anger.

It is important to set limits early in an LBA relationship. Because abusive anger takes its toll on the person on the receiving end, the chances that you will set effective safeguards to protect yourself diminish over time. Each time you suffer an episode of rage, a little bit of your healthy, true "self"—physical, emotional, social, intellectual—is eroded. Victimization is a process that occurs in most cases gradually, but its effects are cumulative. At the point where many victims of toxic anger realize that it is time they engage in self-protective behaviors, they lack both the energy and resolve to do so. A battered woman is not only defined by the physical injuries she endures, but also by her lack of willpower in standing up to her abuser.

Remember Anne (Chapter Four), the woman whose whole sense of self (identity) was destroyed by her tyrannical father while she was still a young child? Children like Anne never have a "fair" chance to defend themselves from toxic anger but adults do. Marilyn, the forty-four-year-old woman we introduced in Chapter One, understood this. "In the beginning of our marriage, I put up with his fits of anger, just tried to ignore it. But, over the years, I learned to separate myself from him when he started to lose his temper. If we were working on something together—like putting a piece of furniture together—I would stop helping the minute he started cussing. I'd simply walk away and leave him to his own misery." You will notice that Marilyn did not try to limit her husband's angry behavior—it was fine with her if he cussed; but she did limit her exposure to such behavior. The same was true when he began to use aggressive language (profanity) around the house: "At first I tried to ignore it. He knew I didn't like it. But that didn't stop him. So I told him, 'You take that back where it came from,' meaning some of his crude angry friends, and he did." Again, what was being limited here was not his behavior, just her tolerance for it.

Another illustration of why it is important to "nip toxic anger in the bud" comes from telephone conversations many people I know have with angry spouses, parents, children, siblings, and loving friends. The story is always the same: the person is upset about having just gotten off the phone with a loved one who has "ranted, raved, and belittled" them. My first question: "How long were you on the phone?" Their (tearful) answer: "Oh, I don't know, about forty-five minutes or so." My second question is: "Why didn't you excuse yourself and hang up as soon as you realized that their agenda was simply to vent anger—like after a minute or two? What possessed you to take it that long?" Their response: "You can't hang up on your mother or your sister; that would be rude." My answer to that: "So, be rude!" It is the same as dealing with telemarketing; if you stay on the line for more than thirty seconds, they've got you.

# What's Keeping Me from Setting Limits?

There are a number of common barriers to effective limit-setting in LBA relationships. These include:

*Codependency*  According to Melody Beattie, author of *Codependency No More*, codependency is the "abandonment of self" that results when a person is so obsessed with controlling the behavior (in this case anger) of those around them that they neglect their own needs, wants, and desires. Codependent individuals are so other-centered that they are selfless. Since their needs are relatively unimportant—including personal safety and health—they do little to protect themselves from harm. In therapy, the codependent client is the one who spends his fifty-minute hour talking exclusively about his angry loved one rather than himself. Any attempt to redirect his attention to his own feelings and/or needs is typically met with stiff resistance or abject silence ("I'm not sure what you want me to say, doctor"). When it comes to anger, according to Beattie, codependent personalities:

- often live with people who are angry

- are frightened of other people's anger

- are afraid of making other people angry

- feel controlled by other people's anger

- have problems experiencing and expressing anger themselves

In addition, codependents: have a hard time saying "no"; tend to perceive themselves as victims; take too much responsibility for the feelings of others; are convinced that their needs/wants are not important; are more concerned about injustices done to others than to themselves; pretend circumstances are not as bad as they really are; watch problems get worse without acting; do not love themselves; seek love and approval "at any and all costs"; equate love with suffering; remain in abusive relationships; have an increased tolerance for adversity; and so on.

How codependent are you?

| 1 | 2 | 3 | 4 |
|---|---|---|---|
| Not At All | A Little | Moderately | Extremely |

Examples:

_____

_____

_____


*The Nonaggressive Style*　　As I noted in Chapter Three, one characteristic of individuals who are predisposed to toxic anger is the aggressive personality style. Similarly, one attribute of people who have a hard time setting limits on anger is the contrasting nonaggressive style. Naomi, for example, rated her ex-husband as a 39 on the APQ, which indicates an extremely high (78 percent) level of overall aggressiveness. Even more noteworthy was the fact that she scored him higher on traits suggesting negative aggressiveness (96 percent) than on those suggesting positive aggressiveness (60 percent). Her ex-husband was extremely impatient, intense, confrontational, demanding, and domineering. But what about Naomi? Her APQ total score at the time she was married was 22, suggesting a fairly nonaggressive style, generally speaking (44 percent). On the negative aggressiveness component, she scored only at the 36 percent level, in sharp contrast to her husband. Naomi was, in effect, the perfect victim counterpart for her bully husband. Now do you understand why it took so long for her to realize that she had to set limits on how exposed she was to her husband's toxic anger?

And what about today? Is Naomi still that nonaggressive or did she change in response to a fourteen-year LBA relationship? I am happy to say that her APQ score now is 30 (60 percent). She will never be the hyperaggressive person that her ex-husband continues to be, but she is certainly not the victim she once was, either. She is determined to never again let herself be in harm's way. Once was enough! Bottom line: "There's a lot of freedom in making the right choices."

Take a few minutes and return to Chapter Three and complete the Aggressive Personality Questionnaire, only this time describe yourself instead of your angry loved one. Maybe you will learn something about yourself that you did not know.

How nonaggressive are you?

| | 4 | 3 | 2 | 1 |
|---|---|---|---|---|
| | Extremely | Moderately | Somewhat | Not at all |
| APQ | (10–20) | (21–30) | (31–40) | (41–50) |

*Fear* Naomi said it best: "Fear goes a long way!" People who are afraid have trouble setting limits. Naomi tried hanging up on her husband when he became abusive on the telephone, but he would leave work and come home to confront her within fifteen minutes, and then his anger would escalate into full-blown rage. People are most fearful when they have been subjected to physical violence. "He only had to hit me one time," Naomi said, "and then he dared me to say anything else. That shut me up." Children caught up in an LBA relationship are more likely to be afraid than adults. Elderly recipients of toxic anger are more fearful than younger victims. Those without resources—money, education, support—are more apt to experience fear when confronted with a loved one's anger. Those with a history of other types of abuse, e.g., sexual, are more likely to be afraid to set limits.

Fear can be a powerful emotion. It paralyzes people, rendering them unable to act in self-serving ways. It overrides logic, reason, and common sense. The primary objective of fear is to escape, not confront. Fear is, in effect, the opposite of anger. It is difficult to stand one's ground (set limits) and run at the same time.

Most of the victims of LBA relationships that I have met were afraid. Jerry is still afraid of his brother, Sam, who he has not seen for seven years. The suspiciousness and cynicism that carries over into all of his relationships with other people, even members of his immediate family, reflect this fear. Sherri is much less afraid of her son's anger than she once was. Donald, a happily married father of three, still cringes in fear whenever his father rages at him. Sarah (who by the way was codependent) was afraid not only of her boyfriend's incessant anger, but also the possibility that he might end the relationship. And Victor actually had to barricade himself in his bedroom to escape his wife's rage.

Naomi discovered a basic truth about herself and those she considered to be her friends: *People react differently to violence.* We/they become fearful and run away. Never was this more evident to Naomi than when her father-in-law came to her upon hearing that she was considering leaving her husband because of his uncontrollable anger. He urged her not to take such action. He was afraid that a divorce would only make his son angrier, and that was something the whole family would then have to deal with. So it is not only our fear that may keep us from setting limits on our loved one's anger, the fear of others with whom we relate and on whom we depend can also serve as a barrier.

**How afraid are you of setting limits?**

| 1 | 2 | 3 | 4 |
|---|---|---|---|
| Not at All | A Little | Moderately | Extremely |

**Examples:**

_____

_____

_____

_____

**How afraid are those around you of your loved one's anger?**

| 1 | 2 | 3 | 4 |
|---|---|---|---|
| Not at All | A Little | Moderately | Extremely |

**Examples:**

_____

_____

_____

_____


*Depression/Hopelessness/Resignation* Depression is an emotional disorder, one that: (1) greatly reduces our energies; (2) leaves us feeling worthless; and (3) interferes with our ability to think clearly and rationally. The more depressed one is, the more this is true. Setting limits on an LBA relationship requires just the opposite—a clear head, enough energy to act in self-protective ways, and a belief that one has value and is worth safe-guarding. Attitudes of hopelessness and pessimism are common in depressed people, reflecting a belief that things cannot improve no matter what one does, so why make the effort? Resignation is the behavioral result of what a depressed individual comes to believe are "futile" attempts to correct a bad situation through his own efforts. A person resigned to his/her own fate does not act.

To see if you are suffering from depression, answer each of the following questions in terms of how you have felt during the past two weeks: (Circle "YES" or "NO" for each)

1. Do you feel sad much of the time?                  YES   NO

2. Do you have trouble sleeping through the night?    YES   NO

3. Do you feel like a "battery that is losing its charge?"      YES      NO

4. Are you gaining/losing weight?      YES      NO

5. Do you have difficulty concentrating or remembering      YES      NO
   things?

6. Do you sometimes cry suddenly for no reason?      YES      NO

7. Do you find yourself not wanting to be bothered      YES      NO
   by other people?

8. Do you have trouble accomplishing routine tasks?      YES      NO

If you answered YES to three or more of these questions, you are probably depressed. Does this surprise you?

*Misguided Beliefs*   In the preceding chapter, we discussed how "myths" about love and anger can impede a person's recovery from an LBA relationship. For most of her marriage, Naomi ascribed to the misguided belief that, "if someone I love gets angry with me, it means I've done something wrong," which is why she tried so hard to be worthy of her overcontrolling, demanding husband. Beliefs guide behavior. If acting wrongly causes one to become angry, then surely we should try to find the "right" way to act.

But Naomi had an epiphany. On that fateful day when she exhausted herself doing something "special" for her husband (beautifying the yard) while he was off having fun with his cronies, only to have him react with scorn and anger, she woke up and realized: "This isn't something I have to put up with; it really isn't. I've done everything for this man and now I realize that even if I do everything for him, he'll never be happy. He's nothing but a spoiled child who wants to get his way no matter what. And anger is how he gets his way."

That was the day Naomi "got her mind right" and began to set limits on her already damaged "self." That was the day she began to heal herself.

*Lack of Resources* Setting limits on oneself sometimes requires external resources. When personal safety is threatened by angry violence, one needs a place to retreat to, a sanctuary. This is why communities have shelters for abused women and children. Family, friends, and neighbors can (and should) also help in this regard.

I had a client, Gwen, who came to me some years back suffering from chronic depression. On our first visit, she cried uncontrollably for forty minutes. When I asked how long she had felt this bad, she replied, "For sixteen years!" It didn't take long to discover the source of her unhappiness—a nonsupportive, selfish, domineering, always-angry husband to whom she had been married for more than a quarter of a century. As we progressed in therapy and Gwen's depression began to lift, her husband became increasingly disturbed by her "new" behavior. She was expressing her own needs, saying "no" to some of his unreasonable demands, making clear her expectations that he treat her better.

The day came (not unexpectedly) when she tearfully told me that her treatment had to end because her husband refused to pay for any further sessions. I reminded her that she was employed and could use her own funds in this regard. In fact, I suggested, this would be another step at limiting the amount of control he exerted over her life. She was overjoyed! Two weeks later, her husband announced that he would no longer drive her to her therapy (she had never had a driver's license), and again she was momentarily disheartened. I reminded her that there were cabs available that could serve as alternative transportation. She happily relayed this to her husband, who then changed his mind (so as to try and maintain at least some control over her). His last ploy was to park his car outside my office window ten minutes before the end of each session, blink his headlights off and on, and play his radio loudly—all attempts to disrupt our conversation. Gwen and I found his childish behavior amusing, we laughed, and stayed to the bitter end.

*Shame/Stigma* People who are victims of toxic anger always feel ashamed. Shame is, in fact, a defining characteristic of being a victim. People who have cancer feel ashamed, people who have AIDS feel ashamed, people who suffer from mental illnesses such as depression feel ashamed, victims of racial discrimination and poverty feel ashamed. They feel undeserving (remember Naomi's statement, "I shouldn't expect more than this (rage) from my husband") of healthy relationships and deserving of the punishment they receive. They are reluctant to share their "secret" of angry abuse, especially from those they love, so they don't talk about their dilemma. Anne (Chapter Five), at age sixty-two, is still trying to resolve the shame she feels for having not been the "absolutely perfect" daughter that her abusive father wanted. Try as she may, even after his death, she is plagued by self-loathing and a fear that others—including close friends—will discover just how "stupid" she really is. Shame is a hard habit to break!

## Step Three: Establishing Boundaries

Each reader must find his/her own way of establishing effective boundaries which will serve as protection from a loved one's toxic anger. Every LBA relationship is different, some more volatile and potentially dangerous than others. Marilyn, for example, was able to set limits on her husband's verbal abuse simply by walking away from any situation once it was clear that he was about to lose his temper. Naomi, on the other hand, had a husband who was so rageful that he would race home to confront her if she hung up the phone during one of his frequent tirades. Strategies that might work for one person might not work for another.

What we can provide, however, are some general guidelines that will fit any situation:

**1. Be a little selfish.** Begin each day spending some quality time with yourself. I spent the majority of my adult life waking up each morning and, as they say, "hitting the bricks running," eager to satisfy all the worldly challenges of the day. And while I succeeded in the short-run, I ended up burned-out, depressed, and in long-term psychotherapy before I was fifty years old. These days, I have a whole new approach to my day. Without exception, I start by eating breakfast at a local family restaurant, where I can enjoy reading my newspaper and my devotional, sit quietly, and nurture myself. What happens after that twenty minutes—including sometimes having to deal with angry people—happens. I figure that since my time, like yours, is valuable, if I spend some of it on myself first thing, I must be valuable, right?

2. **Where possible, love angry people at a distance.** Some of us must endure LBA relationships right where we live, for example, parent-child and marital relationships. These, I believe, are the most difficult when it comes to setting limits. Others, however, can (and I think should) be maintained at a distance. Years ago, some friends of ours had a daughter return home after completing college. They had always had a cordial relationship, but now suddenly their daughter was uncharacteristically angry about every little thing they said or did. Clearly, she was not satisfied about returning home and losing the independence she had enjoyed for four years. Concerned that the hostility between them was escalating and wanting to preserve the "good will" that had once been there, the parents reluctantly came up with a solution that proved quite effective. They evicted her, giving her three weeks to find somewhere else to live. While angry at first, she soon returned to her old loving self after she found her own place. I believe they call this "tough love."

3. **Don't be self-destructive.** Many of you resort to one or another self-destructive habit as a means of coping with the stress imposed by LBA relationships. Smoking, excessive use of alcohol,

overeating, compulsive shopping, prescription narcotics, becoming a workaholic, and abusive exercise are but a few examples. Remember, these behaviors are symptoms of the problem, not solutions.

**4. Keep it simple.** Look for small ways to preserve your ongoing health and well-being. For example, I encouraged one client I had who was in a loving but angry marriage to sign up for some violin lessons. This was something she had always wanted to do for herself, but hadn't because she was too preoccupied with trying to "fix" her husband's bad temper. It did not radically change the marriage, but she was better off. In my earlier book, *Anger-Free: Ten Basic Steps to Managing Your Anger,* I offer more than ninety simple, practical self-help exercises for people who trying to control their anger. These same exercises will work just as well for you. Try them.

**5. Always play it safe.** Never deliberately antagonize someone who is already angry. When I was a small child, my parents fought a lot and inevitably they would get to the point where my father (who had a terrible temper) would try to disengage and leave, at which point my mother would block his way yelling, "You're not going anywhere!" And then he would hit her and leave. As a child hiding under the bed, I never understood why she did that and to this day I still don't.

When anger turns to physical violence, always run to safety and then call the police. Verbal violence is one thing, physical violence quite another. One man who was court-ordered to one of our anger management classes complained because he had "only attacked a window shade that his wife was holding, not her." What, he argued, was the harm in that? I explained to him that "this time it was the blind, the next time it will be her."

**6. Trust your intuition.** Intuition is the "early-warning system" that humans possess that enables us to react quickly to situations that may either benefit or harm us. It is our sixth sense. Most of you get a feeling early on that you are about to be on the receiving end of a loved one's anger, but you often do not act on it right then. You wait until you are sure—facing anger square in the face—and then it's often too late. The damage is done. Trust your feelings and take some type of preventive action, if possible, or at the very least prepare yourself for what you know is coming. Either way, it lessens the impact.

**7. Try counseling.** Modern-day counseling is no longer about lying on a couch recalling events from an unhappy childhood. On the contrary, most therapists spend their time providing support for troubled people who have no one else to reach out to (Step One), helping them discard distorted notions about the world and how one should relate to it (Step Two), showing them how to set appropriate, healthy boundaries (Step Three), and so forth. Many years of working with clients who found themselves mired down in LBA relationships, in fact, provided both the impetus and the step-by-step design of the seven-step program offered here.

Before we move on to the next step, take a few minutes and write down some ways you can set effective limits on your LBA relationship. Remember, these are things you can do *for* yourself, not *to* the angry loved one.

1. _____

_____

2. _____

_____

3. _____

_____

4. _____

_____

5. _____

_____

# CHAPTER TEN

# STEP FOUR:
# DON'T BE A FACILITATOR

LBA relationships are a two-way street. The behavior of each member of the relationship affects and is affected by the behavior of the other. It is, therefore, essential that those of you who love an angry person not act in ways that actually facilitate the continuation and eventual escalation of angry, violent behavior. The dictionary definition of "facilitation" is anything that "makes something easier" or helps something "move forward." As we will see in the following discussion, facilitation for the most part is an active process—that is, it has more to do with what we are doing with and for our angry loved ones than what we are not doing.

## ARE YOU A FACILITATOR?

You may be an anger facilitator and not know it. To find out, I want you to answer the following questions as honestly as you can. Choose one answer for each question and circle the number underneath it.

1. Do you often find yourself saying "I'm sorry" when your loved one becomes angry?

| No | Occasionally | Yes | Absolutely |
|---|---|---|---|
| 0 | 1 | 2 | 3 |

2. Do you keep quiet about your LBA relationship, not sharing your problem with others?

| No | A Little | Pretty Much | Very Much |
|---|---|---|---|
| 0 | 1 | 2 | 3 |

3. Do you tend to minimize the damaging effects your loved one's anger has on you and others?

| No | Sometimes | Often | Always |
|---|---|---|---|
| 0 | 1 | 2 | 3 |

4. Do you find yourself paying the consequences for the anger of someone you love?

| No | Occasionally | Yes | Very Often |
|---|---|---|---|
| 0 | 1 | 2 | 3 |

5. Does your life seem to revolve around your loved one's anger?

| No | Maybe | Yes | Definitely |
|---|---|---|---|
| 0 | 1 | 2 | 3 |

6. When your loved one vents his/her anger toward you verbally, do you hear her out, waiting until she finishes saying every angry thing she can think of?

| No | Not Usually | Sometimes | Always |
|---|---|---|---|
| 0 | 1 | 2 | 3 |

7. Are you more tolerant of anger when it comes from a loved one than from someone you don't love?

| No | Possibly | I Think So | Absolutely |
|---|---|---|---|
| 0 | 1 | 2 | 3 |

8. Do you attempt to help your loved one "save face" after one of his/her angry outbursts?

| No | Occasionally | Sometimes | Often |
|---|---|---|---|
| 0 | 1 | 2 | 3 |

9. Would you say you are "ignorant" about why your loved one is so angry?

| No | Somewhat | Pretty Much | Absolutely |
|---|---|---|---|
| 0 | 1 | 2 | 3 |

10. **Would you say that you have been pretty "nice" about your loved one's anger?**

| No | Possibly | Yes | Too Much So |
|----|----------|-----|-------------|
| 0  | 1        | 2   | 3           |

Now add up your AF scores: _____ If your total score is less than 10, you apparently are doing little to facilitate toxic anger in your loved one. Good for you! If your score falls between 11 and 20, you may well be facilitating unwanted anger. If you scored 21 or higher, like it or not, you are definitely an anger facilitator. The higher your AF score, the more important (and difficult) this step will be for you. Pay particular attention to those questions on which you obtained a score of either 2 or 3.

Remember Mike, the young graduate student we highlighted in Chapter Eight? His AF score was 12. The only two real problem areas had to do with his tendency to *always* hear his girlfriend out when she went on a verbal tirade and to *always* be more tolerant of anger from someone he loved (including others such as immediate family members) than from someone he didn't love. Amanda (Chapter Seven), on the other hand, was a big-time facilitator of anger both as regards her LBA relationship with her alcoholic husband (AF = 24) and her rageful daughter (AF = 21). Her life admittedly revolved totally around their anger; she was always attempting to help them "save face" after their fits of anger; and she was continually saying "I'm sorry" to one or the other. Unlike Mike, Amanda was a big part of her own problem.

# Step Four: Don't Make It Easy for Them

## #1: Stop Apologizing

Some years ago, I realized for the first time that I had a tendency to say "Excuse me" whenever some rude person bumped into me in some public place. Excusing oneself implies that one has behaved wrongly, which I certainly had not. I was, without realizing it, apologizing for their bad behavior. So I stopped saying "Excuse me" and instead now say (loudly) "Excuse you!" whenever someone bulls their way through a crowd and into me. I am always amazed (and amused) at their immediate response, which is to stop instantly, turn and stare at me with a look of utter consternation before resuming their aggressive journey to wherever. I obviously cannot control their behavior, but I can control my own.

The same applies to how you should respond to your loved ones' anger. To say repeatedly "I'm sorry" when they become angry conveys the message to them that you agree that you are responsible for their hostile emotion, not them. Is this the message you really want to send? I hope not. So, either say "Well, *excuse you* for being so angry," if you think you can do this without inviting physical retaliation, or say nothing. Either way, you are better off.

## #2: Silence Is Not Golden

I recall a psychiatrist once proposing a theory that, and I paraphrase, "There are no secrets in life, only conspiracies." I think this is more true than most of us want to believe. AA counselors talk about the alcoholic in the family who is "the elephant in the living room," which no one sees and everyone talks around. The same can be said for LBA relationships.

Let me illustrate this with a story about a recent client. Terri, a young woman in her mid-twenties complained of being extremely angry with her father, who remarried shortly after her mother died of a brain tumor. Her stepmother, it turned out, was a much different personality than her mother, the latter described as sweet, kind, nurturing, and a sort of peacemaker in the family. In sharp contrast, the stepmom was characterized as domineering, critical, defensive, and rather provocative. In an attempt to support her father, Terri initially dealt with her stepmother's anger by keeping quiet and "letting things ride." But this had backfired, leaving her depressed and fighting the pain of repeated migraine headaches. To make matters worse, her father was now burdening her with his own unhappiness about his new wife's hostile behavior rather than confronting his wife directly. Marriage therapists refer to this as triangulation. Terri was in a quandary as to what a "good daughter" should do without continuing to be sick (literally) over the whole mess. I gave her two bits of advice: First, speak up and defend yourself in a nonaggressive manner when your stepmother lashes out at you. And, second, the next time you father comes to you wanting support for what is obviously an LBA relationship, respectfully say, "Dad, I think you're talking to the wrong person. You need to say what you have to say to your wife, not me. Telling me how hurtful her behavior is won't change her. She needs to know how you feel." By triangulating (commiserating) with each other, Terri and her fa-

ther were enabling the new wife to continue her openly hostile behavior. They were both being too silent about what was becoming a
major source of distress in their lives and straining what had always
been a loving father-daughter relationship.

Remember what happened when Naomi went to her husband's
family after her husband became increasingly violent? Did they support her? No. Instead they urged her to enter into a conspiracy of
silence. For years, the family, including her husband, had kept quiet
about her father-in-law's violent temper; now they wanted her help
in keeping quiet about the son's rage. "Do anything but go public,"
they asked. Thank goodness, she didn't listen. I would bet the family is still facilitating her ex-husband's toxic anger. But the good
news is that Naomi is well out of this network of dysfunctional relationships and on to a healthier lifestyle.

The one group of victims that cannot easily "break the silence"
of toxic anger are children. They need adults to reach out to and for
them. Relatives, teachers, and parents of their peers in whom they
confide often serve this important role. What this also means,
though, is that if you are an adult and are not sharing your problem
with others, for whatever reason, you can take it from me: *You are
acting like a child!*

## #3: STOP MINIMIZING

Most of the people I have met and counseled with who suffer from
LBA relationships at first tend to downplay the impact of their loved
one's anger. They use code words like "difficult" to characterize ex-

treme forms of anger (rage) and tend to try and convince themselves (and me) that unless their loved one's anger leads to physical violence it does not qualify as toxic and is not all that harmful. For example, when I initially asked Sherri what it was like having a child who has suffered from uncontrollable rage since early childhood, she would only say, "It hasn't been easy raising him." However, during one of my treatment sessions with her son a few weeks later, when I asked her to talk in detail about the toll his rage took on her over the years—while he had to sit there (at my insistence), look directly at her, and listen without interrupting—her calm demeanor instantly dissolved as she broke down in tears and talked at length about how she had barely maintained her sanity, "hanging on by a wing and a prayer." This rather dramatic outpouring of pent-up emotion made her son more uncomfortable than I had ever seen him, which was good. For a brief moment, I think he actually felt some empathy.

Along the same lines, Anne (Chapter Four) described her tyrannical father as "difficult, very difficult." Sarah (Chapter One) did not see her boyfriend's constant yelling and belittlement of her as rising to the level of abusive anger. And Donald was all too quick to shift the discussion of his father's incessant anger to a recitation of all the good things he had done for the family over the years, as if this somehow mitigated the harm that he had also done.

Do not let your angry loved one off the hook by minimizing the immediate and long-term consequences of his/her anger/violence by saying that things are "okay" when they are not and that you are "all right" when you are most certainly not. Be honest with them.

Follow the sage advice of heralded sportscaster Howard Cosell by "telling it like it is!" Tell them what they clearly do not want to hear—that they have hurt you in every way possible and that they are destroying the love you feel for them.

## #4: Let Them Pay

If one hundred years of psychological science has taught us one thing, it is simply that human beings learn to behave or misbehave as a function of the consequences of their actions. Consequences carry three types of messages: *positive* (your behavior is appropriate, repeat it), *negative* (your behavior is inappropriate, do not repeat it), and *mixed* (your behavior is both appropriate and inappropriate, repeat it). So we do not do our loved ones (or ourselves) a favor by denying them the opportunity of experiencing the natural negative consequences of toxic anger.

Some examples: If your teenage daughter destroys her cell phone during a fit of rage, who should pay for a new phone? Ironically, too many parents feel they should—and they do, absorbing the economic costs of their daughter's temper tantrum. And what about children who do not want anything to do with an angry father after they have suffered his wrath—should the other, non-angry parent intervene and urge the children to "make up" with their father? Absolutely not. A woman has been assaulted by her boyfriend in a drunken rage. Should she try and talk the police out of taking him off to jail? What do you think?

I am not asking you to apply negative consequences to your

loved one's angry behavior, only that you not shield him/her from the consequences that normally follow such "bad" behavior. Can you do that?

**A man prevails on old friends and business acquaintances to give his twenty-eight-year-old son a job. Each time, however, his son loses his temper at work and gets himself fired. The son always comes back to his father, complaining that he was unjustly terminated, and asks his father to help him find another job. What should his father do?**

\_\_\_\_\_ Accept his son's version of why he got fired and call yet another old friend about a possible job for his son.

\_\_\_\_\_ Tell his son that he is no longer willing to help him get re-employed.

\_\_\_\_\_ Other: _____

_____

_____

## #5: GET A LIFE

The stories offered throughout this book illustrate the all-consuming nature of LBA relationships. People live every minute of their waking day anticipating, dreading, and recuperating from an outburst of anger from a loved one. The potential for abusive anger is ever on their mind. Tony (Chapter One), I think, said it best: "Living with my friend, Alan, is like living on top of a volcano. I never know when he is going to erupt next." This is perhaps the most stressful aspect of such relationships.

Sherri, for example, noted how restricted her life was during the years her son was growing up. "I didn't go anywhere where I thought he wouldn't be accepted or it would be too difficult a situation for him to handle," she said. Only now that she has let her son be responsible for his volatile temper (which is helped by the fact that he is no longer in the home) can she begin to have a life of her own. Marilyn feels absolutely free to live her life as she wishes now that she no longer "worries about seeing that angry face" of her ex-husband every time she walks through the front door. And even at this late point in her life, Anne is beginning to develop a life (and identity) of her own now that she is finally out of the shadow of her father's overcontrolling anger. Naomi no longer has to worry about being jerked, hit, or spit on by her angry husband, and Tony no longer has to worry about possibly ending up in the emergency room again simply because he forgot and put something in the wrong place.

Obviously, it is much easier to "get a life" apart from your loved one's anger in situations in which the two of you are physically separated. But what about when you're not? Naomi is a good example. You will remember that, even while she was still living with her husband, she began to rearrange her social life so that she was no longer in that tight circle of family and friends that accepted and condoned her husband's rage. She began to creatively carve out some time for herself and to slowly but surely develop herself as a person, pursuing her own interests and not just satisfying those of her husband. It was, in fact, only in the context of building a separate life for herself that she was able to proceed toward eventually ending the much troubled marriage. The same is true of Lucie, the forty-four-year-old wife of a chronically angry man, who talks about how "scary" it has been to begin "getting a life"—taking up piano lessons again after many years, developing a new friendship with a woman her own age, getting yet another cat (not her husband's thing), which gives her comfort—rather than focusing solely on his wants and demands. "Somewhere in our marriage, I lost sight of who I was and what I wanted my life to be; it was all him." But now that is beginning to change.

**List three things you can begin doing today to redirect the focus of your life away from your loved one's anger:**

1. _____

2. _____

3. _____

## #6: Quit Being Such a Good Listener

There are two good reasons for not being a good listener when a loved one is venting his/her anger: First, as psychologist Aron Wolfe Siegman at the University of Maryland Baltimore County points out, "As people get angry, they experience an increase in cardio-vascular reactions, accelerate their speech, and raise their voices."[1] The angry tone of their conversation increases both in terms of pace (faster) and intensity (louder). There's an escalation effect—as their voice gets angrier, they experience heightened cardiovascular arousal, which in turn fuels an even more intense vocal response.

It's a vicious cycle that feeds on itself. Which me̶
you listen, the more things heat up and the grea̶
harm.

Second, as Siegman further points out, people tend to matc̶
other person's voice style—the louder they get, the louder you get,
and so on. The technical term for this is "conversational congru-
ence or synchrony."[2] The best way not to facilitate your loved one's
anger, then, is to disengage—walk away, hang up the phone—as
soon as you hear the angry tone in his/her voice. The best time to be
a good listener is when he/she is not in an angry mood. I will say
more about this in Chapter Eleven.

## #7: TREAT THEM LIKE STRANGERS

Some years ago, I was involved in a case of an angry young woman
who had severely abused her two children, one of whom was an in-
fant. The youngsters had been taken from her custody and each
year she petitioned to get them back, only to be denied. I recall, the
third year, a court proceeding in which her attorney asked me if I
would be surprised to learn that she was currently working in a
child care facility, responsible for children the same age as her own.
I said "No," to which he replied, "Then if she can take care of
other people's kids all day long without harming them, you must
agree that she is safe to take care of her own." "Absolutely not," I
said, which ignited an angry outburst from the lawyer, who had to
be silenced by the presiding judge. I then went on to explain simply
that people are far more likely to restrain their anger in a public situation with stranger's children than in the private sanctity of their

own home with their own children. Why? Because we have different rules of conduct (and consequences) that govern how we behave with strangers and with loved ones. That's why the vast majority of abuse—emotional, physical, sexual—occurs in so-called "domestic" situations within the context of intimate relationships.

Remember what Sherri said about her teenage son: "There's no one else on this earth that I would stay around for more than two minutes if they treated me the way he does." And remember also that things got better between Sherri and her son once she started treating him like she would anyone else, demanding the same respect, civility, and consideration she would from strangers.

If you would walk away from a stranger who was cussing you in anger, then walk away from a loved one who is doing the same thing. If you would call the police and press charges when a stranger physically assaults you, then call the police when your loved one acts this way. If a stranger came into your home and in the midst of a temper tantrum destroyed some of your property, would you make them pay for the damage? If so, then do the same thing when your son, daughter, husband, or wife breaks things. To do otherwise is to be an enabler.

## #8: Let Them Face Up to Their Anger

Not only should you stop apologizing *to* your loved one every time he/she becomes angry, you should also stop apologizing *for* his/her anger. The first time Naomi helped her husband "save face" after one of his tirades was on that occasion before they got married when she excused his behavior as resulting from too much alcohol.

The friend whom he attacked did the same thing when she accepted his apologies, accompanied by cards, letters, and flowers. After her husband "ripped my shirt completely off me and spit in my face," she again accepted his excuse that he acted this way only because he had been raised by an angry, abusive father who treated his wife and children the same way. "I admit I did feel sorry for him after he told me that and I agreed that he didn't need any professional help," she added. And so it went.

While, as we discussed in Chapter Three, there are many factors that contribute to toxic anger—personality, temperament, substance use, stress—none of these should be used as an excuse for such outrageous behavior.

## #9: Be Smart

When it comes to LBA relationships, what you don't know can hurt you. If you cannot tell the difference between normal, reasonable anger and "toxic" anger, it is unlikely that you will take appropriate action to safeguard your own well-being. Telling yourself that, "Hey, everybody gets angry, right?" is yet another aspect of being an anger facilitator. Reading Chapter Two will help you make this distinction. Also, it is helpful, I think, to understand that the reason your loved one is so angry *has nothing to do with you*—this at least gets you off the hook for their anger. Again, Chapter Three will be helpful. To be ignorant—uninformed, uneducated—at the start of an LBA relationship is understandable; to remain ignorant year after year is foolhardy.

#10: STOP BEING SO NICE

Some of the nicest people I know are victims of LBA relationships. Donald was a nice son to his raging father. Marilyn tried for many years to be nice about her husband's constant anger. Sherri was too nice to her son. Sarah was so nice that she even considered marrying her boyfriend despite his angry mistreatment of her. Victor was a nice husband. Tony continued to act nice despite trips to the emergency room. You yourself are no doubt a nice person—correct? Or have you lost your "niceness" as a function of being in an LBA relationship too long?

Nice people, even though they do not mean to, facilitate abusive anger. They apologize when they have done nothing wrong. They say they are "okay" when they are not. They cry in silence. They accept gifts from a loved one who wants to make amends for their outbursts and assaultive behavior. Nice essentially means agreeable. Are you agreeable with all the angry accusations hurled at you by a loved one during one of their tantrums? Are you agreeable that something you said or did warrants physical abuse?

Nice people also have difficulty setting limits (Chapter Nine). Codependent personalities are typically perceived as nice people. So are passive, nonaggressive persons. And people often act nice when they are afraid. In effect, niceness is a strategy for coping with abusive anger.

If nothing else, I am suggesting that you be at least as nice to yourself as you are to your angry loved one. Being nice to yourself means "getting a life"; it means hanging up the phone on an angry loved one sooner rather than later; it means saying "excuse you" rather than "excuse me"; it means getting a basic education about the difference between normal versus toxic anger—in short, it means not being an anger facilitator.

One last thought: Angry people depend on the niceness of others in order to continue their angry ways.

## What Science Says about Being Nice and Keeping Quiet

More than twenty years ago, I was involved in a study that examined different types of interpersonal "feedback" on aggressive behavior in college students.[3] Students were asked to set varying levels of electric shock for another student with whom they were engaged in a competitive exchange. The higher the level of shock set, the more aggressive their response was considered to be. The exchange was interrupted halfway through and students either: (1) received no feedback whatsoever; (2) heard their opponent matter-of-factly acknowledge that they appeared to be shocking them more than they needed to; or (3) heard the other person respond aggressively, calling them a "jerk" and a "creep." They were then allowed to proceed with the competition. Which group do you think set the highest level of shocks in the second part of the experiment? The first group—the ones who received no feedback from their opponents, who perhaps were just being nice. Surprisingly, keeping one's mouth shut when one is being treated badly appears to be the worst thing you can do. According to this study at least, the best strategy you can employ to lessen the abuse is to acknowledge to the other person that they are treating you in an abusive manner but without personally attacking them "in kind" (Chapter Eleven). The benefit to this approach is that it fosters a sense of empathy on the abuser's part that the other two approaches do not. Remember what happened when I made Sherri honestly recount the toll her son's rage had taken on her in his presence, something she had never done before?

Now on to Step 5—curbing your own anger.

# CHAPTER ELEVEN

# STEP FIVE: TWO WRONGS DON'T MAKE A RIGHT

Toxic anger begets toxic anger. Just ask Marilyn, the woman who never wanted anger to be part of her life: "My husband got angry and it was over quick. But I couldn't let it lie. I wouldn't speak to him for three or four days. And that would make him angry. I know it escalated things, but I couldn't let it be. That wasn't me. I'm not an angry person, but that was my way of making a statement: You're not going to get away with this!"

Marilyn did not begin her marriage being angry. To the contrary, in the early years she did everything but become angry in an effort to "make things right" with her continually angry husband. "It took a lot to make me mad back then," she said, but over time, "I learned to answer anger with anger." However, being angry was never easy for Marilyn, and once angry she had a hard time letting go. Staying angry for days on end was what was toxic about her anger, and what caused her migraine headaches. How does she know this? Simple: she has only had one bad headache in the two years since she divorced her husband.

Marilyn wishes she could have sat and talked with her husband calmly and rationally when he got mad, and she tried. But he would not do his part, so they never resolved the issues that occasioned his anger in the first place. Since he wouldn't do her thing (discuss), she ended up doing his (anger), and that is when the quality of their marriage began to erode.

## Won't I Feel Better?

Since the days of Sigmund Freud, there has been this notion that human beings feel better, relieved, and somehow less victimized when they vent their anger—get things "off their chest," as it were. Research by psychologist James Averill at the University of Massachusetts, however, reveals that nothing could be further from the truth. In a large-scale survey of college students and community residents,[1] Dr. Averill observed that only a minority of respondents admitted actually feeling triumphant (16 percent) or pleased (21 percent) after reacting with anger, in sharp contrast to a majority who felt either hostile (69 percent) or depressed (59 percent) afterward. And almost no one felt "justified" by being angry.

Why is that? Two reasons, I think: To begin with, how one feels after he/she expresses anger is tied to some extent to just how angry they were in the first place. Rage is obviously a much more physically exhausting experience as compared to milder levels of anger such as irritation or annoyance. Second, and even more important, how one feels afterward depends on how he/she expresses the anger. My longtime friend and colleague, Professor Ernest Harburg at the University of Michighan, has demonstrated, for example, that *reflective* anger expression (talking to a person who has provoked you after you have calmed down) is far healthier in terms of one's blood pressure than *resentful* anger expression (protesting angrily to the other person).[2] In this same vein, psychologist Karina Davidson at the Mount Sinai School of Medicine in New York has found that "discussing anger calmly, constructively, and with a motivation to solve problems" reduces one's risk for cardiovascular illness.[3] How do you know if you are handling you anger in a constructive way? Ask yourself the following questions:

- Even though I am angry, am I trying to understand the viewpoint of the other person who provoked my anger?

- Even though I am angry, am I trying to minimize further conflict?

- Am I expressing my anger in a way that allows both sides to eventually come out feeling good?

- After expressing my anger, do I feel closer to a resolution of whatever it was that triggered my anger in the first place?

- After I have expressed my anger, do I feel like things look better than they did at first?

If you answered "yes" to most or all of these questions, you are probably one of those people who, according to Dr. Averill, reports feeling better after you have your say. On the other hand, if you answered "no" to most or all these questions, you are no doubt expressing your anger in a destructive way and you are more likely to continue to feel bad.

Unfortunately, I have found that more often than not human beings choose a destructive means of expressing their anger even though it invariably leads to some harm either to themselves or to others. To illustrate this, I conducted an exercise in a class I was teaching on the topic "Anger in Contemporary America" at a local liberal arts college a couple of years ago. Those enrolled in the class were all honors students. The exercise was simply to write down all the ways in which they expressed themselves when someone—fellow student, professor, girlfriend, parent—made them angry. I was astounded at what I learned. Ninety percent of their responses were negative and included such things as:

- blowing up
- biting the person who made me angry
- screaming
- stomping my feet
- throwing things

- storming off
- grinding my teeth
- being self-critical
- snapping at everybody
- getting into fights

And my personal favorite: "finding a brick wall and kicking it until I can't feel my feet anymore." And, again, these were the brightest, most talented, most creative and resourceful kids in the school! Only a small handful of respondents offered a more constructive way of expressing anger: talking about how she felt either with the person she was mad at or some neutral third party; exercising or going for a walk; and contemplating how best to resolve the problem at hand.

When Dr. Raymond Novaco at the University of California, Irvine, pointed out the various adaptive (positive) functions that anger can serve, such as energizing behavior, causing people to take some action on their own behalf, promoting self-esteem, and, fostering a sense of personal control in stressful situations, he most assuredly was not talking about people who are in a state of rage or those who handle their angry feelings in ways that ultimately prove harmful.[4] He was also not talking about Donald, the middle-aged depressed man (Chapter One), who finally answered his father's rage with rage of his own, yet remained angry and upset many months later. Nor was he talking about Marilyn, whose way of expressing anger in an LBA relationship was to give her husband the "silent treatment" for days on end.

Expression of angry feelings through constructive conversation is good, but what are some other ways to accomplish the same end? Redirecting anger into humor works. Recently, I was having a rather spirited (some might say heated) discussion with someone who finally became so exasperated she angrily told me to "Go to hell!" My first inclination was to answer her anger with an angry response of my own, but instead I simply replied, "No thanks. I've already been there. It's called Galveston, Texas." We both had a laugh, there was a break in the tension, and we then proceeded to resolve our differences. Exercise works, too. I recall getting so angry at my teenage daughter once that I found myself actually contemplating homicide.

Fortunately I was already dressed in my exercise clothes, so instead I just went on to the gym earlier than I had planned. Boy, did I ever have a good workout fueled by all that rage!

And keeping an anger diary works. Professor James Pennebaker at the University of Texas at Austin has found that routinely "confessing" how one feels—especially negative emotions such as anger—by writing in a journal for fifteen to twenty minutes a day prevents anger from escalating over time and has a positive effect on one's physical health.[5] To tell your emotional story, all you need do is write down how you feel without concern for how it reads. Don't judge what you write, just pour out your feelings in an open and uncensored way. This technique may not cure an LBA relationship, but it will also not risk an even angrier exchange with your loved one.

## What Can I Expect When I Get Angry at a Loved One?

What you can expect is that he/she will get even angrier than they already are. I say this in large part based on studies we conducted on school-age children who are asked how they respond if another child gets mad at them. Students are allowed to choose from one of the following three responses:

- Just walk away

- Walk away and return later to discuss why the other person was angry

- Get angry in return—answer anger with anger

The youngsters are first classified as "high anger" or "low anger" respondents, based on their answers to the Toxic Anger Test (Chapter Two). What we learned was that only 18 percent of the least angry children said they would "get angry in return," whereas a whopping 87 percent of the most angry kids chose this option. Equally interesting, I thought, was the fact that none of the most angry children chose to "just walk away," as compared to 38 percent of those who rarely get angry. This is one of the biggest problems I see with pathologically angry children—they simply cannot walk away from an angry exchange. They feel compelled to accelerate the anger-anger process no matter what the eventual cost to themselves or others. What makes them do this? For one thing, the most angry children tend more often to have an aggressive personality style (Chapter Three), that is, they are more confrontational in terms of how they relate to others. For another, these "high anger" youngsters are five times more likely to agree with the philosophy that "anger is about getting even with someone"—in effect, they are more vengeful. Lastly, very angry children actually believe that anger is a good thing (74 percent), whereas other less angry children tend to mostly see anger as something bad (71 percent).

You might ask, "Are these children representative of adults, including those who find themselves in an LBA relationship, who are presumably more emotionally mature?" Actually, they are. In my clinical practice, I find that most of the legal problems stemming from domestic violence arise from anger-anger exchanges that lead to one partner pushing, slapping, or otherwise beating the hell out a loved one. A typical example is a young man whom I was treating for toxic anger who announced as we began our session, "Well, I messed up again!" It seemed he had an angry encounter with his wife, from whom he was separated, which had resulted in his shoving her through a screen door. "I don't know what happened, Dr. Gentry. I was bringing the kids back to their mother. I had just driven up to their mother's house and was getting out of my truck when here she came, storming out the front door, yelling and cussing me for I don't know what. I started yelling back, and the next thing I knew I pushed her away and she fell into the screen door. Then she called the cops and I was arrested for assault and battery." What should the man have done when his wife attacked him? "I should've just gotten back into my truck and backed out of there, right?" Right!

## Anger Management Times Two

Hal and Barbara came to me seeking help for problems they were having with marital communication. Barbara described her feelings about their twenty-five-year marriage as "frustrating and disheartening," when what she really meant was that she was angry at Hal most of the time. Barbara was a rather aggressive personality—demanding and confrontational—whereas Hal, on the other hand, was quiet and somewhat passive. A typical angry exchange would go something like this:

> BARBARA: Did you do what I asked you to do today and go by the
> bank to see about refinancing?
> HAL: (No response.)

BARBARA: (In a tone of obvious irritation) Hal, I asked you if you
  went by the bank today.

HAL: (Again, no reply.)

BARBARA: (Very angry now) Fine! So, I guess you didn't go to the
  bank. I don't know why you can't do one simple thing I ask
  you to do. It's always the same thing. I ask for some help with
  things that need to be done and you won't do your part. (Now
  yelling) I'm sick and tired of this!

HAL: (Retreats into the den where he reads the paper in angry silence.)

Hal and Barbara were both angry, but for different reasons.
Barbara felt totally responsible for everything that went on in the
family and she was constantly feeling overly stressed. It was also
important to Barbara that things be done as she directed them
and on her time schedule. She was a woman of action, and she
expected Hal to respond in the same way. When he disappointed
her (as he often did), she reacted angrily. Unfortunately, Hal did
not like it when he was, as he saw it, "ordered about" by his domineering wife. This stemmed from his having been raised by an
angry, dictatorial father, who treated him much the same way as
his wife. Hal couldn't see that Barbara was his wife, not his father, and that, unlike a child, he had the power (and the right) to
stand up for himself. The angrier Barbara became, the angrier
Hal got. The more aggressive she got, the more passive and with-
drawn he became. She attacked, he retreated. Silence was Hal's
way of frustrating Barbara, of not playing her game—a game of
words and debate which she always won. Thus, the two drove

each other crazy! They were caught in a cycle of anger and could see no way out.

Therapy involved working on both sides of the marital equation. I helped Barbara understand that her need for feedback from Hal was certainly reasonable, but that the aggressive (demanding) way she sought it ensured that it would not be forthcoming. I also helped her develop some empathy for Hal's position by getting him to "open up" about how he felt when she came on so strong and how it reminded him of his angry father. Hal, on the other hand, needed help learning to be more assertive even in the face of Barbara's insistent behavior, rather than taking the easy (and predictable) way out by retreating into silence. Not only that, but it escalated Barbara's anger from irritation to full-blown rage. The crux of the therapy had to do with each of them assuming more responsibility for their own behavior and making the necessary changes instead of using anger as a means of changing (and controlling) the other. After only four visits, the couple reported much improvement in how angry they felt toward each other. Had Barbara come in for anger management therapy alone, with no recognition of Hal's role in "answering anger with anger," I do not believe much would have been achieved. Unfortunately, this is more often the case than not.

## Role Reversal

Don't be surprised if you find yourself feeling a great deal of anger if and when your loved one begins to learn to control his or her temper. This expression of backlogged, pent-up anger in persons who have been on the receiving end of an LBA relationship is one of the unanticipated side effects of successful anger management. Why would you suddenly find yourself feeling angry at a loved one at the very moment when he/she has finally stopped being so angry him/herself? Because you can! In the past, your anger was overshadowed by that of your loved one, waiting only for an opportunity to express itself, and now you have the opportunity. This reversal of roles in an LBA relationship is so common, in fact, that I always alert my angry clients to expect it and not to relapse back into their toxic anger by reacting "in kind." John, the sixty-year-old ex-marine who I featured prominently throughout my earlier book *Anger-Free* is an example. After a lifetime of toxic anger, John has been free of this problem for over a decade now. And, during that time, he has returned to my office many times complaining that his wife is now "angry at me for one thing or another" all the time. His first inclination is, of course, to answer anger with anger, and he almost has on several occasions. But I explained to him that even though this can be a problem, it is normal and certainly no reason for backsliding into his old, angry ways. So what does John do when his wife gets mad at him? He just walks away—incredible for a man who spent the better part of his adult life being physically and emotionally abusive. Getting anger-free is one thing; remaining anger-free is quite another.

But what about John's wife and people like her? What are they supposed to do with their pent-up anger? The first thing they need to do is realize that much of their anger is what I term "old anger," suppressed emotion that is just now seeing the light of day. Rather than reflecting the issues of the moment which supposedly triggered their anger, it reflects old emotional scar tissue formed by countless assaults on their "self" from an angry loved one over the course of time. The second thing they need to do is assess just how angry they are. Has their anger reached the level of being toxic? And, finally, they need to think about forgoing emotional reciprocity—the need to settle the score.

## HOW ANGRY ARE YOU?

Let's take a minute to see how angry you have become as a result of being in an LBA relationship. Answer the same three questions we had you answer in Chapter Two about your loved one's anger, only this time describe yourself:

1. How often during a typical week do you become angry? (Check one)

   _____ Not at all

   _____ 1 or 2 times during the week

   _____ 3 to 5 times during the week

   _____ 1 or 2 times each day

   _____ About 3 to 5 times each day

   _____ More than 5 times each day

**2. On average, how intense is your anger when you get mad? (Circle one)**

| 1 | 2 | 3 | 4 | 5 | 6 | 7 | 8 | 9 | 10 |
|---|---|---|---|---|---|---|---|---|----|
| Mild | | | | | | | | | Extreme |

Now, using the information found on pages 30 to 36, decide which of the 6 anger categories you fit into: (Check one)

_____ Episodic Irritability      _____ Chronic Anger

_____ Episodic Anger      _____ Episodic Rage

_____ Chronic Irritability      _____ Chronic Rage

If you checked any of the three categories on the right, you are definitely *too* angry.

## Step Five: Forgo Reciprocity

Answering anger with anger is motivated by a person's need for emotional reciprocity. That is, we want the other person to feel what we feel. If a loved one compliments us, we feel good, so we compliment them in return so they will feel the same. Similarly, if we are hurt by their anger, we want them to feel just as hurt by ours. Underlying this principle is the misguided belief that somehow this balances things out, settles things, or as they say in the sports business, "creates a level playing field." It does not! Ask yourself: Was Marilyn really keeping her husband from "getting away with" his fits of anger by staying tense and angry herself for several days in a row? Or was she simply producing another migraine headache which would only hurt her, not him—and, more importantly, not change anything about their contentious relationship?

So what does one do instead? The best strategy for coping with another person's anger is to think *response rather than reaction.* Anger typically is an emotional reaction, not a response. A reaction is something that is mindless, something that is highly predictable (an overlearned, habitual, ritualistic way of behaving), that is impulsive and occurs immediately, something that you have no control over—like a "knee-jerk" when the doctor taps you with a rubber hammer. A reaction does not involve the element of choice. A response, on the other hand, is something that is thoughtful, does involve choice, is not always immediate or predictable, and is something that you have control over. What I am suggesting then is that, when you are faced with a loved one's anger, you, in effect, go with your head rather than your heart.

There is a knack to remaining unemotional in the face of another person's anger. I liken it to finding yourself in the "eye of the hurricane," where it is relatively calm despite the fierce winds all around. The last thing you want to do is intentionally step out of the safety of the eye and into the emotional winds of a loved one's rage. This requires an ability to detach emotionally and instead simply be an interested observer of that other person's feelings and behavior. Think of them as an actor on a stage and you are in the audience. You can appreciate what they are doing without actually running up on the stage, can't you? Well, it can be the same here. As

I noted in Chapter One, Sherri learned to do this with her angry adolescent son and their relationship greatly improved.

Once in the eye, ask yourself the following five questions (thus engaging the mind):

(1) Do I want my loved one's emotion to dictate how I feel?

(2) Will I somehow gain an advantage in this relationship if we both lose our temper?

(3) Am I willing to pay the price of my own anger—for example, a migraine headache or being arrested?

(4) Am I "answering anger with anger" because I haven't completed the other steps we have discussed thus far—reaching out for support, getting my mind right, setting limits, and not being an anger facilitator?

(5) Which is more important: my health and well-being or getting even?

If your answer to questions 1 through 4 is YES and getting even is a higher priority, then by all means respond in kind. If your answer to the first four questions is NO and your safety and well-being is your highest priority, then don't.

In dealing with a loved one's anger, I believe it is always better to act than to feel. By "act," I mean removing yourself from harm's way by exiting the situation as quickly as you can. I mean setting limits and effective boundaries (Chapter Nine) between you and his/her anger. I mean desisting from all forms of anger facilitation. I mean engaging in healthy "alternative" behavior, like the example I gave of choosing to exercise at the gym rather than killing my daughter. (Boy, did I get my money's worth that day!) I mean literally anything and everything that comes to mind other than "answering anger with anger," that is not self-destructive, and stands no chance of placing you in greater jeopardy at that moment.

**Write down some example of actions you can take in lieu of answering anger with anger:**

1. _____

_____

_____

2. _____

_____

_____

3. _____

_____

_____

4. _____

_____

_____

5. _____

_____

_____

One last reason for not giving in to the temptation to answer your loved one's anger with anger: the more angry a person is the less hardy he/she is[6] (Chapter Six) and thus the less ready he/she is to meet the challenge of surviving an LBA relationship. Better to be hardy!

# CHAPTER TWELVE

# STEP SIX: STRESS INOCULATION

A loved one's anger, if toxic, can be a source of major distress not unlike divorce, death of a loved one, serious illness, or bankruptcy. Yet, interestingly, you will not find it listed on any of the standard psychological stress measures currently in use. It is the worst type of stressor because it can be *chronic* (persists over time), its effects are *cumulative*, it often seems beyond our capacity for *control*, and—when it involves physical violence or sexual assault—it is considered *catastrophic*.

Obviously, where there is significant stress in a person's life, there is a need for stress management. The strategy most suited for minimizing the harmful effects of toxic anger is a procedure known as stress inoculation training (SIT). SIT is analogous to medical inoculation in which a person is administered a small (controlled) dose of the toxic agent to help enhance his/her resistance, for example, to the smallpox, polio, or flu virus. Inoculation, including in the case of an LBA relationship, is always preventative.

Stress inoculation training was developed more than thirty years ago by Donald Meichenbaum, a psychologist at the University of Waterloo, as a means of helping clients cope more effectively with overpowering anxiety. It has since been used more broadly in the treatment of a wide variety of adverse psychological states (anger, frustration, depression) and physical ailments (headaches, asthma, pain, high blood pressure).[1] Studies using SIT with law enforcement officers (who are regularly the target of angry abuse from citizens), mental-health counselors who often have to deal with angry clients, and victims of various types of traumatic assault (e.g., rape), illustrate the applicability of this technique to the stress inflicted by repeated exposure to excessive anger.

Most of us wait anxiously for our loved one to explode in anger and then defend ourselves as best we can in that moment of rage. One type of defense is denial ("This isn't happening!"); another is simply absorbing the anger ("I'm strong—I can take it!"). Answering anger with anger (Chapter Eleven) is a defensive strategy. None of these maneuvers, unfortunately, provide adequate protection from the damaging effects of toxic anger, and all too often they only compound the problem. Defense is all about trying to escape the inevitable.

Coping, on the other hand, as defined by Dr. Avery Weisman, author of *The Coping Capacity,* is a "strategic effort to master a problem, overcome an obstacle . . . that impedes our progress" along the road of life. It typically involves confronting stress head-on rather than simply trying to avoid or escape it. Coping is proactive, whereas defense is reactive. In other words, it is what you do *before* your loved one becomes angry that does you the most good, not what you do during or after an angry exchange. SIT is a coping technique, not a defensive strategy.

## Step Six: How to Inoculate Yourself

### BECOMING MORE AWARE

Before you can begin to inoculate yourself from the stress of an LBA relationship, you must first become more aware of how you typically react when you are faced with toxic anger. At what point in the interaction with a loved one do you become defensive? Which comes first, defensive thoughts (*Oh please, Lord, don't let her get mad*) or physical reactions (*I can feel tension in the back of my neck*)? How do you behave when your _____ starts becoming abusive with his/her anger? At what point do you begin to have catastrophic thoughts (*Oh my God, I can't stand this!*)? How do you feel after one of these angry encounters: competent (*I think I handled that pretty well*) or incompetent (*It's all my fault. I can't do anything right*)? Most likely, the latter.

Strange as it may seem, you may not be able to answer these questions with any degree of accuracy or precision. Why? Because, as we have noted from the outset, most victims of LBA relationships are much more focused of what their angry loved one is saying, feeling, and doing than they are on themselves. So, in preparation for SIT, you must change your point of focus—to YOUR-SELF.

To begin the process, you do not have to wait for your loved one to lose his/her temper. You can simply sit back comfortably, close your eyes, and imagine the last time you were on the receiving end of an angry exchange. You may be surprised at how easily that image comes to mind. Now, acting as a third-party observer, imagine what you are thinking, how you are feeling, and how you are behaving *in that moment*. Don't be in a hurry. Get as clear a picture as you can of your part of the process. And when you feel like you have gone as far as you can with the image, open your eyes, and immediately write down your observations:

WHEN MY _____ GOT ANGRY, I THOUGHT TO MYSELF: *I hate it when she acts like this.* _____

_____

_____

_____

WHEN HE/SHE BECAME ANGRY, I FELT: *A knot in my stomach.*

_____

_____

_____

_____

**WHEN MY LOVED ONE GOT ANGRY, I REACTED BY:** *I tried to tune him out*. _____

_____

_____

_____

To ensure how accurate your observations are, you may want to compare them with how you actually think, feel, and act the next time your loved one becomes angry. And then you are ready to proceed with your training program.

# Coping with Arousal

The stress of toxic anger comes primarily from the arousal effects it has on your autonomic (emotional) nervous system. Your brain signals your sympathetic nervous system that you are in a threatening situation and—without your knowledge, consent, or control—your heart rate increases, muscles begin to tighten throughout your body, your blood pressure rises, even the hairs on the back of your neck stand up. This is all part of a "fight or flight" reaction, something we humans share with other animals as a built-in means of survival. In the case of repeated exposure to excessive anger, stress thus becomes a conditioned emotional reaction to our day-to-day relationship with a loved one, in effect a "bad habit" that has to be unlearned or deconditioned if we are to remain healthy. Any part of our interaction with an angry loved one can trigger a state of over-arousal. Marilyn, for example, became tense every time she came home just anticipating the angry look on her husband's face when she opened the door. She was already on the defensive, prepared for the worst and paying a price for impending anger, before the two even had a chance to say hello.

There are two ways to counteract stress in an angry exchange: The first has to do with positive self-talk in which the person who is on the receiving end of the exchange tones down their usual level of arousal by repeating certain phrases to him- or herself which have the opposite, calming effect. Examples include:

*"I can handle this. I've been through it before, many times."*

*"Easy does it. Don't get rattled."*

*"There is no point in my getting mad. Two wrongs don't make a right."*

*"She may not be in control, but I am."*

*"That knot in my stomach is normal under the circum-stances. If I relax, it will go away."*

*"Emotions come and go—even anger. I just have to be calm and wait it out."*

*"I'm not taking this personally. His anger is not about me."*

*"I have a lot of things I want to accomplish today. React-ing to anger will only get in my way."*

*"What I do here is more important than what he/she does."*

*"I need to stay relaxed, relaxed, relaxed."*

The other has to do with directly activating what notable stress re-searcher Herbert Benson calls the *relaxation response*.[2] According to Dr. Benson, this built-in antidote to stress can be triggered sim-ply by breathing in and out through your nose, easily and naturally, while silently repeating the word "one," or some other word such as "peace" or "relax," on the out-breath. The key is to practice the technique daily so that you can employ it effectively when you are faced with another person's anger. Let's try it:

1. Sit quietly in a comfortable position.

2. Close your eyes to avoid distractions.

3. Do not try to make yourself relax. This will have the oppo-site effect. Instead, maintain a passive attitude and permit re-laxation to occur at its own pace.

4. Breathe through your nose. Become aware of the natural ebb and flow of your breathing. As you breathe out, say the word "one" silently to yourself. Breathe in . . . out, "one"; in . . . out, "one"; and so on.

5. Continue this for ten minutes. If necessary, you may open your eyes to check the time.

6. When you have finished, continue to sit quietly for several more minutes, at first with your eyes closed and then with them open. Do not stand up for a few minutes.

7. Ask yourself: "How do I feel now as compared to before I tried the exercise? Did I relax?" The answer will almost always be yes.

## What to Do, What to Do?

The final thing one needs to do in SIT is to *generate situation-specific solutions* to the other person's anger. These have to do with nondefensive, nonantagonistic behaviors you can engage in to maintain personal safety, prevent the escalation of anger, and, if possible, to achieve some type of constructive closure on your loved one's anger. For example, you might simply acknowledge their anger by stating the obvious, followed by a question—"I can see you are very angry. What I'm having trouble understanding is, why?"—and doing so in a reasonable tone of voice and without critical comment. Or, you might ask, "It must be terribly uncomfortable to be *that* angry. Is it?" The hope is that such a comment will cause them to reflect on their own angry behavior rather than on you as both the cause and target of such feelings.

Another technique is to decide henceforth to always let your angry loved one have the last word, only you decide when that is. I found this response to be quite effective years ago when my adolescent daughter and I were having far too many angry exchanges. I remember, after one particularly distressing exchange, putting myself in the role of the third-party observer and "getting a visual" of the step-by-step process by which she and I escalated into our usual shouting match. What I quickly realized was that we were both (she's too much like me!) trying to have the final word as a way of winning the debate over whatever issue had provoked my/her anger in the first place. I also realized that since we both couldn't win the struggle, one of us had to be a loser. Finally, I realized that my daughter was less prepared to lose than I was. So I decided, from that point on, always to let her have the last word, but to let that happen early on before we both got too angry and went beyond the point of no return. The next time (a few days later) we found ourselves in an angry exchange, as soon as I felt myself getting overly aroused (tense), I gave in and simply said, "Hey, I'm about to lose my temper here and I don't want that to happen. So, I'm going to stop now and go do something else. If you want to come back and discuss this later when we've both calmed down, that's fine. Let me know" and then I walked off. My daughter was stunned because I wasn't playing the usual "anger game," and the first couple of times I responded that way she followed me, trying to continue the argument, to no avail. In no time, we were no longer engaged in an LBA relationship and we could talk more openly and freely about legitimate "points of disagreement" without finding ourselves in a win-lose battle. The key here is that I first had to imagine myself responding in this "new" way before I could actually behave that way in the real world in which I lived. (By the way, we have a beautiful relationship today. We've both done a lot of growing up since.)

Take a minute and write down a few "specific" things you can do the next time you are confronted with your loved one's anger:

1. *I can* _____

_____

2. *I can* _____

_____

3. *I can* _____

_____

4. *I can* _____

_____

5. *I can* _____

_____

The way you inoculate yourself from stress is to rehearse how you will cope successfully with a loved one's anger by intentionally putting yourself in that situation through the use of imagery and reinforcing your belief that you can, as we said in the previous chapter, be the "eye of the hurricane." Most of you have spent all of your time doing just the opposite, avoiding thinking about your loved one's anger until you are faced with it. You are ready to defend yourself from the other person's wrath, but not to adequately cope with it. Each time you rehearse—train yourself—it is analogous to giving yourself yet another inoculation against undue stress. The more you rehearse, the greater your resistance! I recommend that you set aside time every day for SIT, which for those of you in LBA relationships should be considered just as important as brushing your teeth, bathing, eating, taking out the trash, and as any other "routine" daily activities.

## Reflection and Reinforcement

There are essentially two goals with SIT: (1) to remain task-oriented and problem-solve when dealing with anger from a loved one rather than reacting emotionally—sad, hurt, or angry; and (2) to be aroused without becoming overwhelmed. Reflect on the last time you were involved in an angry exchange and ask yourself this question: "Am I meeting these goals?" If you are, then reward yourself in some small, meaningful way. Treat yourself to lunch with a friend. Buy yourself some fresh flowers. Brag to a confidant how well you are doing. Pat yourself on the back and say, "Good for me! It couldn't happen to a nicer guy." Celebrate.

When victims of LBA relationships describe situations in which they are confronted with toxic anger by a loved one, I frequently suggest constructive behavioral alternatives to their normal ways of defending themselves. Their response is always the same: "Darn, I wish I had thought to say or do that." Step Six—inoculating yourself—is just about that, preparing yourself for what to say and do differently so that something comes to mind when you need it. It's about preparing yourself to cope effectively instead of being victimized. Sherri brought her teenage son to me for anger management training, but in the process she learned how to cope better with his toxic anger. Both benefited, but what she learned to do on her own was actually more helpful to her in the long run than what I was able to teach her son. Sherri learned that her emotional destiny was more in her hands than she realized, and it was at that point that she began to free herself from her son's outrageous behavior.

# CHAPTER THIRTEEN

# STEP SEVEN:
# WHEN ALL ELSE FAILS

Obviously not every LBA relationship will survive. Invariably, it is the non-angry partner who takes the initiative in ending such relationships, typically as a result of having suffered well beyond reason. Unfortunately, far too many reach this point without having gone through the various steps that we have outlined in this book, having exhausted themselves instead by trying in vain to "fix" their angry loved one. Remember Victor, the man who endured and assuaged his wife's relentless anger for over a decade by keeping silent, avoiding her, being logical in defending himself against her accusations, and finally barricading himself in his bedroom? After all that, one day he just decided to divorce her, and he did. But while that decision may have been inevitable, had Victor been able to reach out to others, set limits, and incorporate stress inoculation training into his daily routine, maybe he would not have been so emotionally devastated that day he first walked into my office.

The other reason for going through a multi-step process leading up to a possible transition out of an LBA relationship is that you will be better prepared for a "life after toxic anger" and also so that you do not spend your time and energies second-guessing your decision to move on with your life with lingering doubts about "What if I had only . . . ?" and "Maybe, if I had just . . . ?," wondering if somehow things would have turned out differently. In short, working through the first six steps allows you to make a "clean" break, if that is what it comes to.

## IS IT TIME TO TRANSITION?

To help you more objectively decide whether it is time to consider transitioning out of an LBA relationship, answer each of the following questions honestly:

1. Does your loved one suffer from pathologic anger as described in Chapter Two?
   YES (2)     NO (0)

2. Have you and do you continue to suffer significant damage as a result of loving this angry person?
   YES, I continue to (2)    YES, I have in the past (1)    NO (0)

3. Have you reached out to others for help in dealing with this LBA relationship?

   YES (1)     NO (0)

4. Have you "gotten your mind right" regarding the relationship between these two strong emotions: love and anger?

   YES (1)     NO (0)

5. Have you set effective limits on your own tolerance for abusive anger?

   YES (1)     NO (0)

6. Have you stopped being an anger facilitator?

   YES (1)     NO (0)

7. Have you stopped "answering anger with anger" in dealing with your loved one?

   YES (1)     NO (0)

8. Have you made stress inoculation training a part of your daily routine?

   YES (1)     NO (0)

9. Do you always feel "unsafe" when you are interacting with your loved one?

   YES (2)     NO (0)

10. Has your angry loved one physically assaulted (pushed, slapped, hit, kicked) you in the past thirty days?

    YES (3)     NO (0)

11. Do you have financial resources, if necessary, to sustain you in transitioning out of an LBA relationship?

   YES (2)      NO (0)

12. Have you explored the legal ramifications (as well as your legal rights), if necessary, before ending the LBA relationship?

   YES (2)      NO (0)

13. Do you feel "strong" and "well" enough to begin a transition out of your LBA relationship?

   YES (2)      NO (0)

14. Do you have sufficient social support to see you through this transition in your life?

   YES (2)      NO (0)

15. Are you prepared to deal with continuing anger on your loved one's part even after you end the relationship?

   YES (2)      NO (0)

Now add up your points: _____ Then divide your point total by twenty-five and you will get a percentage score, telling you how ready you are to make a successful break from a relationship that can only do you further harm. For example, if your total score = 10, your percentage score is 40. If your score is 19, your percentage score is 76.

My percentage score is: _____ percent

If your percentage score is less than 50 percent, there is either no need for you to terminate your relationship with an angry loved one or you are not ready to do so. In the latter case, obviously there is much work left to be done. If your percentage score is between 50 and 70 percent, you are acknowledging the fact that this relationship continues to be a dangerous one but that you are well on your way to "getting out of harm's way." Good for you! If your percentage score is above 70 percent, you are nearing the point where a clean break is possible.

## Tony Makes a Clean Break

In Chapter One, you will remember I described Tony as a young man in the painful process of trying to make sense out of a long-standing LBA relationship with his partner, Alan. I spent the one day I had to counsel with Tony helping him: (1) appreciate the fact that his loving partner did indeed suffer from toxic anger; and (2) see that he should begin to look after himself more instead of trying so hard to "fix" the relationship. Well, it turns out that was all he needed to begin what turned out to be a two-year process of eventually ending this relationship.

"After we talked, I began to look at myself for a change," he said in a recent telephone conversation, "and I didn't like what I saw."

Tony was also appreciative that I had recommended that he read Belva Plain's fictional account of an LBA relationship in *Whispers*,[1] because it reminded him of his own family growing up and how the relationship he had with Alan was a re-creation of the one he had had with his "loving but angry" father. He also recognized that he had taken on the role of his mother, who had always been strong and "made things come out right in the end" even in the face of his father's episodic rage. And, while neither he nor I felt the need for him to spend years in psychoanalytic therapy reliving these early family relationships, it did give him sufficient insight into his own behavior to realize that a change was definitely in order.

The two years Tony spent between the time we met that once and when he finally parted company forever with Alan was, however, well spent. In effect, he began to work his way through the various steps we have discussed—finally realizing just how pathologic Alan's anger was, reaching out to others for support, rethinking his attitudes about anger and love, and most of all continuing to prepare himself for a life that no longer centered around the fear of toxic anger—until he was ready for the biggest and most difficult step of all. He began a regular program of exercise, found himself a new apartment that was free of the "old memories of anger and abuse" and where he also felt safer, and he began a new business which brought a lot of new excitement and challenges into his life to balance out some of the damage done by his relationship with Alan. Tony already knew that he had to break it off with this man, whom he still loved, but these new "selfish" activities made him feel emotionally stronger, more independent, as well as more confident about himself. "I just took it one step at a time," he explained, "but I got there eventually."

Tony is happier now than he has ever been in his whole life and he no longer feels so intimidated by the world around him. Why? Because Alan (and Alan's anger) is no longer the center of that world. Tony is in a new relationship now, one that—like all relationships—is by no means perfect, but does not involve toxic anger. He and his new "easygoing" partner can talk openly and intimately and, on occasion, even "agree to disagree" without risking the possibility of rage. Tony sees his new partner as an ally, not an adversary, which means that he need not be on the defensive all the time they are together. This no doubt explains why the severe temporomandibular joint (TMJ) pain he experienced when he was with Alan has now virtually disappeared. Not wanting to find himself in yet another LBA relationship, Tony was clear from the outset about the limits of his tolerance for unfair treatment even with someone with whom he chose to share his life. Daily life is more predictable and tension-free for Tony now, and he feels like he can cope with most of what comes his way in the future, now that so much of his physical and psychic energies are not being constantly siphoned away to defend himself from someone else's outrage. Most of all, Tony believes he can now continue to grow as a unique and healthy person, something that was not possible before.

## Another Success Story

Like Tony, Naomi, the young woman I introduced in Chapter Nine, found happiness after ending an LBA relationship with her ex-husband. Unlike Tony, however, it only took her nine months to make the transition once she realized that her husband's angry behavior was "not something I have to put up with for the rest of my life." Again, the transition involved a series of small steps. First, she began to dissociate from the inner circle of friends and family that facilitated her husband's outrageous behavior. Second, she began to fashion an increasingly independent lifestyle, e.g., getting a part-time job which also allowed her to accumulate some money of her own, which she realized she would need after she broke up with her husband. Third, she began taking better care of her health by avoiding as much as possible the stresses that triggered her migraine headaches. Fourth, she restructured her thinking about her husband by realizing that anger and violence were not the actions of a loving adult but rather those of "a spoiled child." Along these same lines, Naomi also began to think that living free of fear and intimidation was much more essential than "living with material things." She was willing to relinquish some of her comfortable lifestyle in ex-change for true happiness and personal safety, something she could see other friends who were in LBA marriages unable to do. As she put it: "Not being oppressed anymore makes everything else seem less important." In effect, Naomi had replaced her angry husband's "checklist" with one of her own, one that would prepare her for life after toxic anger.

Naomi finds herself a happy person these past eight years, de-spite some residual (post-traumatic) sensitivity to anger and vio-lence. "I still have trouble coping with my children fighting—what amounts to normal sibling rivalry—because I'm afraid where it will lead. I also don't watch violence on television or so-called action movies with my kids," she adds. "I've had enough of that already in my life." Naomi feels grateful for having a second chance at life, and she no longer has that feeling of hopelessness that she had for fourteen years of marriage. "I no longer walk around all day think-ing 'what not to say' to set my husband off, always being afraid." She is truly liberated.

One of the biggest ironies in her life is that members of her ex-husband's family continue to call her about how abusively he treats them. Naomi listens dispassionately, now that she is, as they say, "on the outside looking in" at a family terrorized by a very angry man.

## From the Frying Pan into the Fire

Not all transitions out of LBA relationships have a happy ending. All too often, victims of such relationships find themselves ending one angry partnership only to begin another. Charles is an example. I had seen him briefly in therapy some years ago, right after he had separated from his wife whom he described as having an "out of control" temper and being physically violent at times. Like Victor, Charles had tried everything he could think of to assuage his wife's recurrent rage, only to see her worsen over the years. When I first met him, he was severely depressed, lonely, and in great need of support for the transition he was making out of his marriage. I pro-vided that support, as well as validated the fact that his wife by all accounts did suffer from toxic anger, apparently fueled by a major mood disorder that had gone untreated. When I last saw Charles, he seemed to be doing well.

And then, four years later, he showed up back in my office, re-peating the same sad story as before. Only this time, it was with his new wife, who, as it turns out, is an equally hyperaggressive woman (she scored 47 on the APQ)—confrontational, demanding, dominant—and is as verbally abusive as his first wife had been physically. Charles had jumped from the proverbial frying pain into the fire! He found himself right back where he was the first time I saw him: depressed, stressed (heart palpitations), exhausted, unable to relax or sleep, and entertaining periodic thoughts of suicide. What struck me the most was his sense of utter bewilderment about how he could have gotten himself back into another LBA relationship. The good news was that Charles was reaching out for help, which as we now know is the first step in the process toward recovery.

# A Word about Sadness

You cannot end an LBA relationship without feeling sad. Sad because of the emotional investment you made in a relationship that was doomed from the start by your loved one's toxic anger, and sad because of what might have been. Jerry makes a conscious effort not to think or talk about his angry brother, Sam, who he has not seen for seven years, lest he feel sad. The sadness is right under the surface and is readily apparent as soon as he begins recollecting their early years together. Sherri feels sad when she sees how cordial her friends' relationships are with their sons and she thinks to herself, "Oh, my, wouldn't that be nice?" Donald is sad about being alienated from his angry father in the later years of his life. Sarah is sad when she occasionally thinks about ending her relationship with the first love of her life, a young man she was fully intent on marrying. And, as crazy as it may sound, Naomi is sad for her ex-husband for all that his anger has cost him (including their marriage), not to mention her children who have been third-party victims of their father's abusive anger.

With normal, uncomplicated loss, sadness is usually short-lived. The sadness that accompanies the termination of LBA relationships, however, sometimes lingers because it is mixed with other feelings such as guilt, anger, fear, and alienation. Sometimes anticipation of this sadness can be a barrier to ending an LBA relationship, and quite often—because it lingers—sadness can turn into depression. When either of these is the case, you need to reach out for professional counseling.

Life is often about tough choices. If you are forced to choose between sadness and fear/intimidation/oppression, by all means choose sadness.

# EPILOGUE

Self-help books, no matter what their respective content, share one common purpose—to help human beings take personal responsibility in the affairs of everyday life. This is no less true when you have the misfortune of loving a very angry person than it is when you must look for a "plumber's guide" to assist you in repairing a leaky faucet. If you, the reader, do not come away with this single, powerful message as it applies to minimizing the damage inflicted through LBA relationships, then I have failed as a writer.

But I am confident that this will not be the case for two simple reasons: (1) the inspiring "real person" stories of husbands, wives, girlfriends, sons, daughters, parents, and brothers who have managed to find a greater measure of freedom, safety, health, and happiness both within and outside such relationships; and (2) the seven "tools" offered to make this happen in a reasonable and effective way.

Tony perhaps said it best: "When I came to see you Dr. Gentry, my life was totally out of control, thanks to the abusive behavior of my partner. You were the first person who ever asked me what I wanted to do for myself. You challenged me to look to myself for change instead of continuing to focus solely on that other person. You gave me permission to become a stronger person, both physically and emotionally, and you taught me that it's OK to do what's good for me for a change. Since that day, I have, more and more, lived life on my terms."

Tony is certainly not unique. He is but one of millions of people who struggle valiantly with loving but angry relationships day in and day out. His story can, if you want, be your story—with the same positive outcome. It's all about you, and it's all up to you. Good luck.

# NOTES

## CHAPTER ONE: YOUR LOVE, THEIR ANGER

1. R. Williams and V. Williams, *Anger Kills: Seventeen Strategies for Controlling the Hostility that Can Harm Your Health* (New York: Time Books, 1993).
2. "Fact Sheet," Colorado Coalition Against Domestic Violence, Internet site, *www.psynet.net/ccav*, 1998.
3. Surgeon General, United States Public Health Services, *Journal of American Medical Association* 276, no. 23 (1992): 3132.
4. J. G. Silverman et al., "Dating Violence Against Adolescent Girls and Associated Substance Use, Unhealthy Weight Control, Sexual Risk Behavior, Pregnancy, and Suicidality," *Journal of American Medical Association* 286, no. 5 (2001): 572–579.
5. 20/20, "Battle of the Sexes–Spousal Abuse Cuts Both Ways," Internet site, *www.abcnews.go.com/sections/2020_batteredhusband030207.html*, 2003.

## CHAPTER TWO: HOW ANGRY IS *TOO* ANGRY?

1. P. Ekman and W. V. Friesen, "Constants Across Cultures in the Face and Emotion," *Journal of Personality and Social Psychology* 17 (1971): 124–129.

2. J. R. Averill, "Studies of Anger and Aggression: Implications for Theories of Emotion," *American Psychologist* 38 (1983): 1145–1160.


## CHAPTER THREE: WHY ARE THEY SO ANGRY?

1. A. Caspi et al., "Continuities and Consequences of Interactional Styles Across the Life Course," *Journal of Personality* 57 (1989): 375–406.

2. C. J. Wilkinson, "Effects of Diazepan (Valium) and Trait Anxiety on Human Physical Aggression and Emotional State," *Journal of Behavioral Medicine* 8 (1985): 101–114.

3. D. R. Cherek et al., "Regular or Decaffeinated Coffee and Subsequent Human Aggressive Behavior," *Psychiatry Research* 11 (1984): 251–258.

4. C. Ague, "Nicotine and Smoking: Effects Upon Subjective Changes in Mood," *Psychopharmacologia* 30 (1973): 323–328.

5. W. J. Rejeski et al., "Anabolic Steroids and Aggressive Behavior in Cynomolgus Monkeys," *Journal of Behavioral Medicine* 11 (1988): 95–105.

6. E. Harburg et al., "Negative Affect, Alcohol Consumption, and Hangover Symptoms Among Normal Drinkers in a Small Community," *Journal of Studies on Alcohol* 42 (1981): 998–1012.

7. J. Borrill et al., "The Influence of Alcohol on Judgement of Facial Expressions of Emotion," *British Journal of Medical Psychology* 60 (1987): 71–77.

8. I. M. Birnbaum et al., "Alcohol and Sober Mood State in Female Social Drinkers," *Alcoholism: Clinical and Experimental Research* 7 (1983): 362–368.

9. J. M. Gottman and R. W. Levenson, "Marital Processes Predictive of Later Dissolution: Behavior, Physiology, and Health," *Journal of Personality and Social Psychology* 63 (1992): 221–233.

10. J. M. Gottman et al., "Parental Meta-Emotion Philosophy and the Emotional Life of Families: Theoretical Models and Preliminary Data," *Journal of Family Psychology* 10 (1996): 243–268.

11. S. Monroe, "Major and Minor Life Events as Predictors of Psychological Distress: Further Issues and Findings," *Journal of Behavioral Medicine* 6 (1983): 189–205.

## CHAPTER FOUR: STOP THE ANGER

1. J. J. Gross et al., "Emotion and Aging: Experience, Expression, and Control," *Psychology and Aging* 12 (1997): 590–599.

## CHAPTER FIVE: DAMAGE ASSESSMENT

1. I. Kawachi et al., "A Prospective Study of Anger and Coronary Heart Disease. The Normative Aging Study," *Circulation* 94 (1996): 2090–2095.

2. J. G. Silverman et al., "Dating Violence Against Adolescent Girls and Associated Substance Use, Unhealthy Weight Control, Sexual Risk Behavior, Pregnancy, and Suicidality," *Journal of American Medical Association* 286 (2001): 572–579.

## CHAPTER SIX: IS IT POSSIBLE TO CHANGE?

1. J. O. Prochaska et al., "In Search of How People Change: Applications to Addictive Behaviors," *American Psychologist* 47 (1992): 1102–1114.

2. A. Bandura, *Self-Efficacy: The Exercise of Control* (San Francisco: W. H. Freeman, 1997).

3. S. Kobasa, "Stressful Life Events, Personality, and Health: An Inquiry Into Hardiness," *Journal of Personality and Social Psychology* 37 (1979): 1–11.

## CHAPTER SEVEN: STEP ONE: REACHING OUT

1. R. B. Williams et al., "Prognostic Importance of Social and Economic Resources Among Medically Treated Patients with Angiographically Documented Coronary Artery Disease," *Journal of American Medical Association* 267 (1992): 520–524.

2. K. B. Nuckolls et al., "Psychosocial Assets, Life Crisis and the Prognosis of Pregnancy," *American Journal of Epidemiology* 95 (1972): 431–441.

3. J. S. House, "Barriers to Work Stress: I. Social Support," in *Behavioral Medicine: Work, Stress, and Health,* ed. W. D. Gentry et al. (Boston: Martinus Nijhoff, 1985), 157–180.

## CHAPTER EIGHT: STEP TWO: GET YOUR MIND RIGHT

1. A. Ellis, "Changing Rational-Emotive Therapy (RET) to Rational-Emotive Behavior Therapy (REBT)," *Journal of Rational-Emotive and Cognitive-Behavior Therapy* 13 (1995): 85–89.

## CHAPTER TEN: STEP FOUR: DON'T BE A FACILITATOR

1. A. W. Siegman et al., "The Angry Voice: Its Effects on the Experience of Anger and Cardiovascular Reactivity," *Psychosomatic Medicine* 52 (1990): 631–643.

2. S. Feldstein et al., "A Chronography of Conversation: In Defense of an Objective Approach," *Nonverbal Behavior and Communication, 2nd Edition,* eds. A. W. Siegman and A. W. Feldstein (Hillsdale, NJ: Erlbaum Associates, 1978).

3. T. Gaines et al., "The Effect of Descriptive Anger Expression, Insult, and No Feedback on Interpersonal Aggression, Hostility, and Empathy," *Genetic Psychology Monographs* 95 (1977): 349–367.

## CHAPTER ELEVEN: STEP FIVE: TWO WRONGS DON'T MAKE A RIGHT

1. J. R. Averill, *Anger and Aggression—An Essay on Emotion* (New York: Springer-Verlag, 1982).

2. E. Harburg et al., "Resentful and Reflective Coping with Arbitrary Authority and Blood Pressure: Detroit," *Psychosomatic Medicine* 41 (1979): 189–201.

3. K. Davidson et al., "Constructive Anger Verbal Behavior Predicts Blood Pressure in a Population-Based Sample," *Health Psychology* 19 (2000): 55–64.

4. R. W. Novaco, "The Function and Regulation of the Arousal of Anger," *American Journal of Psychiatry* 133 (1976): 1124–1128.

5. J. W. Pennebaker, *Opening Up—The Healing Power of Expressing Emotions* (New York: Guilford, 1990).

6. M. T. Johnson-Saylor, *Relationships Among Anger Experience, Anger Expression, Hostility, Social Support and Health Risk,* Unpublished Dissertation, University of Michigan, 1986.

## CHAPTER TWELVE: STEP SIX: STRESS INOCULATION

1. D. Meichenbaum and M. E. Jaremko, ed., *Stress Reduction and Prevention* (New York: Plenum, 1983).

2. H. Benson, *The Relaxation Response* (New York: William Morrow, 1975).

## CHAPTER THIRTEEN: STEP SEVEN: WHEN ALL ELSE FAILS

1. B. Plain, *Whispers* (New York: Dell, 1994).

**W. Doyle Gentry, Ph.D.,** is an author, educator, scientist, consultant, and clinical psychologist whose career spans thirty years. His scholarly work—which includes over 100 professional and scientific publications—is cited as an authoritative source by top anger researchers. He lectures and gives workshops extensively both in the United States and abroad. He is editor-in-chief of the prestigious *Journal of Behavioral Medicine,* a post he has held for over twenty-five years.